NEXT LEVEL BODY AND SOUL DIGEST

Douglas S. Harvey

Trilogy Christian Publishers
A Wholly Owned Subsidiary of Trinity Broadcasting Network
2442 Michelle Drive
Tustin, CA 92780

For information, address Trilogy Christian Publishing
Rights Department, 2442 Michelle Drive, Tustin, Ca 92780.
Trilogy Christian Publishing/ TBN and colophon are trademarks
of Trinity Broadcasting Network.
For information about special discounts for bulk purchases,
please contact Trilogy Christian Publishing.
Manufactured in the United States of America

10 9 8 7 6 5 4 3 2 1
Library of Congress Cataloging-in-Publication Data is available.
ISBN 978-1-64773-853-2
ISBN 978-1-64773-854-9 (ebook)

This book is dedicated to Dana—my sister, daughter of the King, my friend and wife. And to all people who wish to enjoy a long healthspan and to know the fullness of God's Spirit in their everyday lives, just as the people enjoyed in biblical times.

ACKNOWLEDGMENTS

All endeavors in life are a partnership. A partnership with the living God of Abraham, Isaac, and Jacob, and with the people in our lives. So it has been with the writing of this book, which would not have happened without the active participation of both. Nonetheless, first and foremost, nothing of value is accomplished in the kingdom of heaven apart from Jesus ("Apart from Me you can do nothing," John 15:5 NLT), and the anointing of God the Holy Spirit (Acts 1:8 NLT, "But you will receive power when the Holy Spirit comes upon you.").

These acknowledgments are not in order of significance, for all played a vital role in this work. Much gratitude to Jonathan and his wife Tracey for their encouragement, direction, and refinement of the book title and content. Along with Cathy, who assisted the writer in many of the administrative duties necessary for publication, along with the professional team at Trilogy and their promotion of the work.

With many thanks to the three women (Nicole, Jessica, and Cynthia) who, without solicitation, said this book would be written. Along with Elizabeth, Heidi, and Madonna, members of the "Wellness Team" at LifeExtension, for their professionalism and research materials and their passion to see all pursue "the science of a healthier life."

With gratitude to all the men of RAMBF (Rockwall Area Men's Bible Fellowship) for allowing me to serve them and enjoy their brotherhood in Christ for many years. Along with Ben for his many "Healthier Temple" series, including the one on fasting used in this work. Also, to John for designing the bookmark to use as a constant reminder. And lastly, to Thomas and his daughter Kathy, for their help with corrections on the manuscript.

TABLE OF CONTENTS

INTRODUCTION

This book is designed to invite you to consider the great value of our bodies and our souls. The two are married together in a critical way that affects our wellbeing and the purpose for which we are made.

The author's wish is for you to see that the choices that we make concerning our bodies can have immediate and long-term positive and negative consequences. The first half of this book will demonstrate that most of the signs of aging and disease are caused by the choices we make—not our genes. This will be demonstrated to you through documented stories and leading scientists and medical doctors in their fields of study. This will encourage and empower the reader that we are not victims in the lottery of the gene pool. Furthermore, this book serves as a "digest" to introduce you to these leaders for your future reference, so that you may stay informed.

The second half of the book is the most important part of the book—and our lives. Namely, the present and eternal nature of our souls. Most people do not realize that everyone is going to live forever; but, as they say in real estate, "It's all about location, location, location"!

At the same time, all of us have a "soul hunger" that we want to be satisfied. The things we seek to feed that soul hunger are mostly filled with empty calories. We need to go to the super-foods that will fill our soul hunger. Many of us have been wandering back and forth from the buffet table of religion and the church for a long time and have missed out on the fine foods that satisfy the soul—without unnecessary calories!

SECTION ONE:
The Body

WHY BOTHER WITH THE BODY?

◆ ◆ ◆

❝Why?" can be a good place to start when beginning a discussion. Namely, why do we do what we do? When we know the "why," it can better motivate us to continue in our desired direction. Dr. Kenneth Cooper, who is best known as the "father of aerobics" and founder of the Cooper Clinic in Dallas, Texas, makes a great statement that we all need to hear: "It is cheaper and much more enjoyable to maintain good health than it is to regain health once it is lost."[1]

The key word that is noteworthy is *enjoyable*. Many medical doctors would echo the same message to their patients. They see all the consequences of poor lifestyle choices and the resulting health problems. Not to mention the emotional toll—the needless pain and suffering that is experienced because of premature disease. The writer has had conversations with doctors he is acquainted with, and they have shared with him that they see this all the time. For example, someone comes into their office with a complaint with a medical problem, and they want a pill to make the condition disappear. Many times, they are obese, smoke, do not exercise, and give no thought to their diet and nutrition. They ask the doctor for some prescription (a magic pill) that will make all their symptoms "go away." There is no such pill that will make up for good choices.

An ancient Hebrew prophet stated: "My people [God's people] are destroyed from lack of knowledge."[2] If individuals were aware of the connection between premature aging and disease, they would make better choices as to what they put in their bodies. In the chapters that follow, we will discuss many of the factors that highly increase the risk of damage to our bodies—opening a door to disease and aging them prematurely.

LIFESPAN
AND HEALTHSPAN

◆ ◆ ◆

There are five "Blue Zones," as they are called, on our planet. They provide a model for us of both a long lifespan and a functional healthspan. These five "Blue Zones" are: Sardinia, Italy; Okinawa, Japan; Loma Linda, California; Nicoya Peninsula, Costa Rica; and Ikaria, Greece. The author uses the phrase "functional healthspan" intentionally, because these five groups of people not only live the longest, but more importantly, they live the longest functional life—without disability! Some individuals you and I know live a long life, but most do not function well. That is not the case here in these communities, as we shall see!

There is a saying: "Ignorance is bliss, until the consequences come." Only the foolhardy would dismiss the lessons one can learn from these individuals who have mastered the art and science of living well! These are not theories on healthy and long lifespans, but living testimonials that validate what works. It is the way of wisdom. Jesus said it best: "But wisdom is shown to be right by its results."[3] When one has the preponderance of evidence that shows what works, it is the way of wisdom to take note!

There has been an argument against lifestyle choices—genes. To cut to the chase, genes have been much overemphasized, to the point that individuals believe that the choices they make about lifestyle have no bearing on their health, falsely believing that their genes have been cast in stone. This is not the case, however! As it is humorously said, "That dog won't hunt, and that bird don't fly"!

In her book *Younger*, Dr. Sara Gottfried makes the statement: "The scientific reality is that 90 percent of the signs of aging and disease are caused by lifestyle choices, not genes."[4] Dr. Gottfried's statement is also affirmed by Dan Buettner, the author of *The Blue Zones*. Mr.

Buettner affirms the power of choice when he states: "Since lifestyle, not genes, is the chief determinant of how we live... Blue Zone(s) offer the world's best practices in health and longevity."[5] This fact should encourage you and empower you at the same time. You and I are not victims; we have the power of choice! Choice is one of the gifts of our Creator. We are free to make wise choices that will sustain and maintain this wonderful body that our Creator has given us to last a full lifetime, free to function as it was designed! As you reflect on that fact, it raises a very important question: given the fact that you and I have the personal power to choose a healthier lifestyle, why would we not want to make choices that will make us feel, look, and function better?

We are not left alone to our own resources. We can ask our Creator, who is the ultimate Source and Resource for whatever help we may need to make good choices. Just pray a simple prayer for help; He promises His strength to help us make wise, healthy choices and much more, as we shall see!

Centenarian Wisdom

In Dan Buettner's book *The Blue Zones*, he uses a term called "centenarian wisdom." He states: "These are individuals... that are the healthiest, and longest-lived people. They have many things to teach us about living longer, richer lives. If wisdom is the sum of knowledge plus experience, then these possess more wisdom than anyone else."[6]

The writer has selected two of many stories from *The Blue Zones* that will give you a real-life sample of individuals who have mastered the art and science of living long and well!

Marge Jetton

Marge is a lady who stands out in Dan Buettner's library of individuals who are one hundred years old and are still going strong. She resides in Loma Linda, California. She has already celebrated her one hundredth birthday and is a practicing Seventh Day Adventist. There is a picture of her in Mr. Buettner's book with a big smile on her face, with outstretched arms holding two dumbbells as part of her workout routine. She rides a stationary bike between six and eight miles and between twenty and twenty-five mph each day except on the Sabbath. She also begins her day with a one-mile walk. Marge says, "I'm for anything that has to do with health."[7]

Marge rarely eats meat and eats lots of veggies. Yet there is much more to her strategy than diet and exercise. People are a key ingredient to her joy of living. She states, "I found that when you are depressed, that's when you do something for somebody else."[8]

Two other observations you can make as you read about Marge's lifestyle are that she appreciates nature, and that she takes the Sabbath seriously. Marge says, "Ah, the roses," leaning forward into a brilliant red trio of them. "I can't look at a rose without thinking of Jesus. When I was a girl, we used to go on long family walks on the Sabbath and look at all the wildflowers." The Sabbath is, as Marge puts it, "a time to come apart from the things of the world. It is something to look forward to."[9]

Stamatis Moratis

Now we travel to another part of the world, to "look into the window" of another man's life, who is one hundred and fully functional. Stamatis's story began in Florida, where he was living with his family. He was a house painter contractor who developed a good reputation for doing excellent work. His reputation earned him the opportunity to paint Rose Kennedy's house.

As Dan Buettner reports: one day at work Stamatis, now in his early 60s, felt short of breath and noticed he was getting fatigued easily, to the point that he could not complete a full day's work.

Consequently, Stamatis went to the doctor; they took x-rays and concluded that he had lung cancer, most likely from inhaling all those paint fumes for many years—and his three-pack a day habit of smoking sure did not help the situation. Four more doctors confirmed the diagnosis, as Buettner recaps the story. The doctors gave him six to nine months to live.[10] Stamatis thought about remaining in Florida, where he could receive cancer treatment. He reasoned that a funeral in Florida was much more money than in Ikaria, Greece, where his elderly parents still resided. So, Stamatis and his wife decided to move, and went to Ikaria to live out his remaining six to nine months.

When they arrived, Stamatis rested at his parents' humble home. After a short time he began to venture outside, enjoying the legendary sea breezes and fresh air. He began going to church and "got religion," as Buettner states. More specifically, though, Ikaria is a committed community of Greek Orthodox Christians. Stamatis got himself up on Sundays and went to the chapel and got more than religion—he got Jesus! His lifestyle was changing. Stamatis got to reconnect with old friends, tending a garden near his house and eating the native cuisine, which we will summarize later.

Ikaria is a mountainous terrain with many slopes and hills. All of the locals walk and hike the terrain, as people have for centuries. This activity forced Stamatis to get regular, daily exercise.

Interestingly, after living in Ikaria for decades now, Stamatis is one hundred years old. Mr. Buettner interviewed him while he was visiting Stamatis in Ikaria. Buettner went back to the United States and called Stamatis on the phone with some follow-up questions. One was most noteworthy: "Stamatis, did you ever go back to the States to find out what happened to your cancer?" "Yes," said Stamatis. "About ten years after my diagnosis, I went back to see the doctors." "What did they say?" said Mr. Buettner. "Nothing," said Stamatis. Incredulously, Buettner responded, "Nothing? Why?" Stamatis stated matter-of-factly, "They (the doctors) were all dead!"

Ida Keeling

We go back to America to meet an extraordinary woman who created her own "Blue Zone" right where she is! Dr. Sara Gottfried cites Ida in her book *Younger*. Dr. Gottfried mentions that she found Ida Keeling on Facebook. In her picture, Ida was doing a push-up with a big smile, with defined deltoids. Ida is known for saying, "Never use age as an excuse." And she is living by this motto. Ida is a record-holder in track for the hundred-meter dash. Along with running, Ida bikes, jumps rope, and goes to yoga twice per week. You say, "So what?" Well, Ida is one hundred years old! Moreover, she did not start running until she was sixty-seven years old! She keeps going, even with a mild case of arthritis. Ida provides one of the secrets to longevity and quality of life when she states, "Exercise is one of the world's greatest medicines."[11]

It all started with Ida making a choice during a difficult period in her life. Two of her sons had died as a result of drugs. Ida was depressed as a result of the loss of her boys. Then one day, her daughter invited her to run a 5K with her. Ida hesitated, but said to herself, Why not; it cannot hurt. That simple step forward changed Ida's life forever.

Ida has written her own story, with her picture on the front cover of her book—smiling. Smiling because she is a follower of Jesus Christ. Ida knows firsthand that when we accept the gift of salvation from Jesus and let Him take the driver's seat, He will lavish us with renewed joy, purpose, and a sense of well-being that we could never imagine! The title of Ida's book is significant: *Can't Nothing Bring Me Down*, subtitled: *Chasing Myself in the Race Against Time.*

The Take-Away from Three Centennials

All three are engaged in daily exercise. Being sedentary is considered the new smoking (one must be insane to smoke). The body shuts down when sedentary; it was designed for physical activity as Marge, Stamatis, and Ida have clearly demonstrated. In addition to helping your body stay strong and function better, exercise also affects your brain in a very positive way. Namely, even moderate exercise increases dopamine levels. Dopamine is the "fun chemical" or the "do it again" chemical. It is a neurotransmitter that is released by neurons (nerve cells) to communicate with other nerve cells. This is all stimulated by exercise, which elevates our mood and acts as a catharsis to rid the body of negative energy and stress. Exercise tricks the body and brain in a positive way by making it function as our Creator designed it to function. It also staves off depression and disease, as we have seen in these three remarkable and yet ordinary individuals who engage in this practice regularly.

All three centennials have a vibrant relationship with the Lord Jesus. They are connected to the family of faith. They actively participate in their churches. Moreover, Christianity is more than a religion to them. Christ is the prominent Person in their personal lives, which has ramifications for their public lives and how they view their purpose here on planet earth.

TEMPLE HEALTH

◆ ◆ ◆

One of the prayers the writer often prays when saying "grace" over his food is: "Bless this food to my body and this body to Your service." The writer heard a friend and his wife pray this prayer when giving thanks for their food. It is powerful, because it lines up with what the Bible says about our bodies: "Don't you know that you yourselves are God's temple, and God's spirit lives in you?"[12] The apostle Paul continues with an even more cogent point when he states: "Do you not know that your bodies are temples of the Holy Spirit, who is in you, whom you have received from God? You are not your own; you were bought at a price. Therefore honor God with your bodies."[13]

Interestingly, this Scripture is rich with

meaning. First, St. Paul employs two rhetorical questions in these passages with the implied answer: "Yes, I know." This Greek grammar is not used by Paul as a guilt trip, but as "joyous elation"! Paul is overjoyed with the fact that the Holy Spirit, who is very God of very God, lives inside all professing Christians! The apostle Paul, writing Holy Scripture, is giving us the foundation for why we should treat our bodies well, and he states his case enthusiastically since it is good news!

One of the writer's friends, Ben Waller, who has been in the healthcare field for over twenty years, gave a presentation to our men's Bible fellowship with these bullet points:

- Our bodies were created in the image of God.

- They are a gift from our heavenly Father to allow us to experience mortality and continue to become more like Him.

- This knowledge influences the way we treat our bodies and how we feel about our heavenly Father and ourselves.

- When we treat our bodies as temples of God, we obtain physical, emotional, and spiritual blessings.[14]

An Adversary of your Health

A few years ago, my friend's wife was diagnosed with cancer. She received treatment, and thankfully, the cancer went into remission. I asked my friend, "How do they check to see that the cancer has gone into remission?" He stated matter-of-factly, "They scan the area of body in question and inject it with glucose. If there is still cancer present, it lights up on the scan since the cancer feeds on the glucose"—sugar!

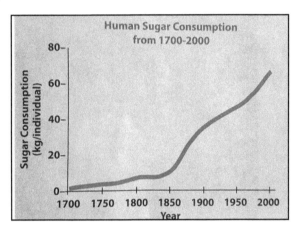

15

As one can observe from the chart, human consumption of sugar has spiked dramatically—with ensuing diseases—at a alarming rate. Many health care professionals are beginning to realize that sugar is not fit for human consumption. Moreover, it is even toxic to our bodies. In the 1700s the annual rate of sugar consumption was around four pounds per year; now it's around a hundred pounds per year![16]

Consequently, there has been a rapid increase in obesity, cancer risk, and even heart disease due to chronic inflammation.

LifeExtension makes a cogent warning that we all need to hear. They state, "We at Life-Extension advise cancer patients to stop all simple sugar consumption and cut back on glucose-spiking starches like rice, bread, and other wheat/corn products."[17]

The message that personal choice of diet has a critical role for children should make moms proactive and involved in the food choices that their young children make. This is a serious issue. Why, you say? Most people do not think of children and cancer as common. Well, it is more common than any mom or dad should want for their child. As Dr. Joel Fuhrman states, "Excluding accidents, cancer is the leading cause of death in children younger than fifteen."[18] His argument is that there is a great lack of veggies and fruits in our children's diets. As a consequence, children are eating more and more "fast food," including sugary foods which have dire consequences for us and our children!

As you can see from this ad, there was a time when cigarette smoking was so prevalent that even doctors were part of the narrative, implying that it was harmless.[19] Likewise, refined sugar is marketed the same way in so many processed foods and sugary beverages. Advertisers, and the addictive nature of refined sugar, and the unwillingness of many healthcare professionals to sound the alarm, have created a toxic mix that is highly addictive and can cause short- and long-term negative consequences to the human body.

Interestingly, in March of 2018, JAMA (the Journal of the American Medical Association) classified almost 40 percent of Americans as obese. This is alarming of course, with all the functional years of human life cut short due to heart disease, type II diabetes, hypertension, increased risk of stroke, and many cancers. However, what is more disturbing is that not enough healthcare professionals are warning people of one of the primary causes of the obesity problem—refined sugar!

There is a reason for this: money, and a lot of it is at stake. The sugar industry is powerful and has money that affects medical research. As Dr. David Perlmutter stated, "We were sold a bill of goods over thirty years ago, and we realize now—after a recent publication in JAMA, on the front page of The New York Times—that the reason doctors were parroting this 'low fat, low fat' was because of the sugar industry influencing the data that was reported in the late 1960s, and that stuck like glue."[20]

The takeaway from this discussion is that we all like sugar, and it sells. Food manufacturers put sugar in many things we consume and many beverages we drink. We must limit our intake of these sugary, processed foods and drinks. Rather, go to whole foods like fruits that are naturally sweet and are loaded with antioxidants and phytochemicals (which we will discuss further, later) that our Creator placed by design on this earth to feed and fuel the bodies He created to function as He intended!

True Health Care Is Self-Care

The above quote comes from Dr. Joel Fuhrman's book *Fast Food Genocide*; he is a leader in diet and nutritional science. The title at first glance may seem melodramatic, but the writer assures you that it is well-documented with the latest scientific research to validate his recommendations. It will open your eyes to the fact that no one watches your body and the bodies of your loved ones as you do. The operative word here is "science"; these are "not old wives' tales" or "snake oils" that are being peddled. As a matter of fact, Doctors Joel Fuhrman, Sara Gottfried, Nicholas Perricone, David Perlmutter, and Kenneth H. Cooper are the top pioneers and leaders in diet and nutritional science. It would be advantageous for you to become familiar with these authors. This is one of the author's goals—to compile a very abbreviated form of some of their important recommendations that will vastly improve your life and the lives of your loved ones!

All of these authors that the writer has cited have impeccable credentials. They are all saying the same message in their books: that your health is directly determined from lifestyle choices and not your genes. Genes, as they are, play "a" role, not "the" role.

Environment, diet, and nutrition play the biggest roles in your health and optimal function of your body! All of us have "good" genes and "bad" genes. The lifestyle choices we make can switch on these bad genes prematurely. Dr. Fuhrman goes so far to make his claims through many years of research and clinical experience. He states that the following can be diminished or even reversed through diet and nutrition:

Prevention of high blood pressure and even reversal in many cases

Prevention of type II diabetes and even reversal in the vast majority of cases

Prevention of heart attacks and even reversal of advanced heart disease in the vast majority of cases

Prevention of breast cancer, prostate cancer, and colon cancer if adopted early enough in life, and even reversal in many cases of early cancer

Prevention of childhood cancer and autism

Improvement in overall health, intelligence, and emotional stability[21]

You ask, and rightly so: Why do I not hear more about these types of statements and claims from my doctor? All of these protocols cited cost little money and are noninvasive to your body and life indeed.

Dr. Kenneth Cooper is president and founder of the Cooper Aerobics Center in Dallas,

Texas, which includes the Cooper Clinic and the renowned Institute for Aerobics Research. Dr. Cooper is acknowledged as an international leader in the health and fitness movement. His programs are used by professional athletes as well as the military. His resume is extensive, with his medical degree and a master's in public health from Harvard University.

You ask, why all this background information on Dr. Cooper, and what does it have to do with my health? The writer is so glad you asked that question. We live in a culture where all opinions are seemingly treated as equal. Some of this is due to social media. All opinions are not equal. There are individuals in the medical community who are the leaders in their profession due to the quality of their education and clinical training, and their desire to continue to research and develop their knowledge of medicine, including the science of diet and nutrition.

Add to this the critical issue of integrity. Integrity is demonstrated when it admits it does not know something, and admits that one has had little training in the subject matter, without money influencing the counsel that is given. Dr. Cooper, speaking on the National Day of Prayer, which is the first Thursday of every May, shared the following story with the audience that makes the point well.

When he graduated medical school, he was sharing with his colleagues that he was thinking of going into preventative medicine. Their response was revealing: "You do not want to do that—there is no money in that." This, unfortunately, is not something to laugh about! This is one of the issues that must be navigated in our medical community. Much of conventional medicine is incentivized by money, and not by prevention.

Well, you say, that is just one event; unfortunately, no. The writer has several MDs as friends, and he has heard stories like this before. One comes to mind. This MD was in a group practice, and his colleagues said to him, "There is always some procedure you can find to perform." My friend left that practice and later opened his own private practice.

The writer's intent is not to paint all MDs with a broad brush. Nonetheless, one should be discerning as to whether treatments are motivated by money. All of us can be corrupted by greed; every one of us has been infected with a virus called sin.

Peak Performance for Your Body

Food is more than fuel. Food has powerful potential for good or bad; the consequences are not always immediate, yet the foods we choose to eat impact the body in a powerful way. Many of our mothers and grandmothers said, as we were growing up, "You are what you eat." These words were profoundly true and wise, even before we had all the modern science we now enjoy.

The author remembers as a young teen his grandmother serving fish at her home. This was many years before we had the wealth of nutritional information we have today. She would say, with her homespun wisdom, "Douglas, you do not hear of Eskimos with heart disease, do you?" The implied answer to her rhetorical question was a definite no. This is not a "fishy story"—pun intended. You may start complaining, "I do not like fish—I tried it once, and it didn't work for me." Well, let me encourage you again to give one type of fish fresh consideration, with an appeal to your vanity as a motivator.

The Brain-Beauty Connection

Now that your attention has been heightened, I will explain. Nicholas Perricone, M.D., in his book *The Perricone Promise*, clearly lays out how one can look younger and live longer. Part of his thesis is that there is a brain-beauty connection. He is not talking about the IQ score per se. Rather, that if one is maintaining a healthy diet that is healthy for one's brain, it will also manifest in healthy and beautiful skin. How is that possible, you ask? Well, there is a connection to the health of your skin and the health of your brain. If you remember your middle school basic science, your largest covering, which we call skin, is also the largest organ of your body!

Consequently, when our brains are healthy from diet and nutrition, the beauty of our skin glows and shows this fact. You may ask: What specifically makes our brains healthy, boosting our cognition and making our skin look good as well? The answer and protocol are provided by our Creator. He provides whole foods that are nutrient-rich in phytochemicals and antioxidants which are not found in processed foods and fast foods. Our Maker provides foods that fuel and sustain our bodies as He designed them to function. He is our Source and Resource for an abundant life, which includes our bodies that He designed.

The problem arises when we do not consult the "owner's manual" He has provided for optimal function and longevity. The Bible states: "Then God said, 'I now give you every seed-bearing plant on the face of the entire earth and every tree that has fruit with seed in it. They will be yours for food."[22] These plants contain life-giving nutrients called phytochemicals and antioxidants. Phytochemicals are biologically active compounds found in plants. Additionally, antioxidants are substances that inhibit oxidation in living organisms; they combat "free radicals"—unstable oxygen molecules that wreak havoc on our bodies. According to Dr. Ken Cooper, "Free radicals are molecular outlaws that travel through your bloodstream, and they have been implicated as the cause of more than fifty diseases."[23] Antioxidants are like the Avengers, the superheroes that wage war against these "villains," free radicals, that travel through the superhighways of our bloodstreams into our cells and attack them! But the Sovereign Avenger, who thoughtfully designed us by His "R&D," equipped us to feed and fuel our immune system to war against these free radicals by energizing our bodies with antioxidants to combat these devils of destruction!

Dr. Cooper cites six specific benefits of supplementing with antioxidants:

1. Increased protection from many forms of cancer
2. Stronger defenses against cardiovascular disease and stroke

3. The prevention of cataracts

4. A delay in premature aging

5. A more powerful immune system

6. A decreased risk of early Parkinson's disease, and many other major health advantages[24]

We saw this earlier as we explored a few individuals in what are known as the "Blue Zones." They enjoy long, functional, peak performance by eating a plant-based diet that consists primarily of vegetables, fruits, beans, nuts, and seeds, with meat as a condiment—not the main course!

Eat and Enjoy Your Medicine

Earlier we quoted Hippocrates (c.460-377 BC), the Greek physician known as the "father of medicine," from whom the medical profession's Hippocratic oath originates. He is famous for the statement, "Let food be thy medicine and medicine be thy food."

Our Creator created whole foods for our health and enjoyment. They are fruits, vegetables, nuts, and seeds. Not processed foods in a box that have a longer shelf life than your grandfather's false teeth! Manufactured foods are highly processed, calorically dense, and nutritionally void of antioxidants and phytochemicals.

You may say: "So what—this stuff tastes good." Indeed, the food manufacturers know that the best bait to place on the "lure" to hook us is taste. However, this creates a cycle of addiction and cravings. Consequently, because one is consuming these empty calories, there is no place for these richly colorful vegetables and fruits that contain life-sustaining antioxidants and phytochemicals.

Super Foods That Affect Longevity
One does not hear of Eskimos having cholesterol or heart problems. Why? They eat fish—and large quantities of it. Many believe that Eskimos benefit from the large amounts of omega-3 fatty acids in the fish they eat.

Moreover, the writer has never heard of or

seen anyone who is obese from eating too much fish. On the contrary, one will find that those who willfully choose not to have fish in their diet many times are overweight, which leads to other health problems. Fish is a lean source of protein that has the additional benefit of satisfying your appetite, making one feel full.

The type of fish you want on your shopping list is cold-water fish, not farm-raised. The types that are best, with low levels of mercury and other toxins, are smaller, wild-caught fish like wild Alaskan salmon, bass, cod, and trout. The "champion" of the super-food of fish is red salmon, also known as sockeye salmon. The deep red pigment gives sockeye its nutritional status.

Dr. Nicholas Perricone cites some reasons why this super-fish is so vital to have in our diet on a regular basis. Dr. Perricone states four important factors:

1. Salmon is the heart-healthiest high-protein food of all.

2. Salmon is unique among protein foods in that it is powerfully anti-inflammatory.

This is because salmon is by far the best source of long-chain omega-3 essential fatty acids (EPA, DHA, and others).

3. Salmon is the richest food source of a uniquely powerful antioxidant, an anti-inflammatory orange pigment called astaxanthin.

4. Salmon is a rare dietary source of DMAE, the natural human neurochemical proven to help improve muscle tone in the face, thereby reducing wrinkles.[25]

Idiot-Proof
Everybody is busy today with work, family, and household responsibilities that place a felt squeeze on our food preparation time. Moreover, some do not possess the skill set to cook fresh or frozen fish on a regular basis. There is good news: canned fish is perfectly acceptable. All that is necessary is a can opener—some cans come ready with a flip tab to open. Most cans are now labeled as "Non-Intent BPA," but if contents are not used after opening, they should be stored in a separate container and re-

frigerated.

Many good sources of cold-water fish are canned and ready to eat. They are red and pink salmon, sardines, and anchovies. All of these fish are good sources of omega-3 fatty acids and are an excellent source of lean and clean protein. No worries about cooking the fish properly; it's "idiot-proof"!

Veggies for Vitality

Veggies rock! You say, what's the excitement about veggies? That is a great question. Remember that we discussed the "Blue Zones" earlier? Well, the common ingredient, among other things, is veggies—lots of them, with a rainbow of colors. The deep rich colors of green, yellow, orange, and red are packed with antioxidants and phytochemicals also sometimes called phytonutrients (which are biologically active compounds found in plants).

Dr. Joel Fuhrman cites some of these important compounds found in plants and the benefit to our brains—which most people want to keep!

These compounds are phytochemicals such as lycopene in tomatoes, isoflavones in soy, and flavonoids in fruits. Dr. Fuhrman continues by stating the benefit to our brains: "Phytochemicals affect brain development, brain function, and brain pathology."[26] This should only reinforce the importance of feeding our children veggies and fruits at a very early age. Once introduced into their diets, this should become a lifelong, prominent part of their food choices throughout adulthood. Our brains are very sensitive and crave phytochemicals to function at their optimum levels with good cognitive function—not to decline! This gives our children an IQ boost from the beginning and keeps their brains (and more) healthy, so they can achieve all that the Lord intended them to do! Why would a parent place their young child or teenager at a disadvantage in life by feeding them a diet of processed food that is calorically dense, yet void of vegetation that is rich with antioxidants and phytochemicals?

Fast food is highly addictive and results in individual lives being cut short, which is a human tragedy. Processed food is void of brain and body nutrients and is highly addictive by design. Food advertisers and marketers have no intentional malice toward their customers. Food purveyors are selling "taste and convenience," and that sells; however, it comes at a cost to our children's and our own health. Dr. Fuhrman's book packages this vital information very cogently. The subtitle of his book provides a wake-up call to all of us to the harmful effects of "fast food." The subtitle: *How Processed Food Is Killing Us, and What We Can Do About It.* One can extrapolate from his book and other leaders[27] in the scientific field of diet and nutrition that there are negative consequences to not eating vegetables, such as being more prone to addictions (drug use), crime, and mental illness. This is not set in stone, however.

Conversely, there are positive consequences (immediate and long-term) to eating a diet rich in vegetables. Students can expect better academic achievement, alertness, and attention span when they consume "high octane" vegetation for their brain. Marry that with omega-3 fatty acids as we described earlier, as it feeds their brain cells with the much-needed compounds to enhance memory and mood and protects the brain from cognitive decline. It makes getting that grade a little easier!

Some antioxidants and phytochemicals have not even been discovered yet. They are hidden treasures, placed there by our Creator and the Sustainer of our bodies to promote health and fight disease. Veggies will keep you lean and mean with muscle when they are partnered with regular exercise. You will not get fat eating veggies; it will not happen. Moreover, you will have more energy, and you will look and feel younger and age more slowly in your adult years.

Dr. Sara Gottfried, in an interview with Pat Robertson on *The 700 Club*, shared that she eats one to two pounds of veggies per day. She practices what she tells her patients, and it shows. Dr. Robertson even commented that she looks decades younger than the age on her license! The writer would concur; she did look decades younger (her book is called *Younger*) than her given age. This sounds like a lot of veggies, but isn't really when meat is the condiment of your meal and not the focal point.

As men, we are usually more carnivorous than women. Men like meat! Meat is not bad or evil; it just should not be the dominant feature of our meals and diet, as we have seen through the study of the people who live in the "Blue Zones" who have the longest functional health. This diet also improves our energy levels, combating fatigue and making us more productive, with less down time being sick.

KEEPING IT
SIMPLE

◆ ◆ ◆

Everyone is so busy today. Students, working moms, dads, and even the retired complain that they are busy! For this reason, it is a challenge to eat one to two pounds of veggies per day so that we can function well, as so many people do in the "Blue Zones" that we discussed earlier.

The author has mixed a veggie cocktail that is full of vegetables and is idiot-proof with its simplicity. All one needs is a blender and organic veggies, and in less than ten minutes, you can drink your veggies. What makes it so convenient and healthy is that you are not juicing; you are using the complete veggie with all its fiber. You just add water—filtered water, preferably—and then hit the power button, and you're finished!

What goes in this energy booster? A garden variety of veggies that you can tweak to your taste buds. My cocktail includes frozen, organic broccoli, corn, and peas. Then fresh, organic kale, organic celery, organic carrots, a small amount of onion, and organic green apples for sweetness. The water is key to the consistency and enabling the veggies to blend smoothly. You will need a decent blender with some "horsepower" to blend these veggies together efficiently!

One can store any unused product in the fridge for up to twenty-four hours. It is best to use it up within that time for maximum benefit. It would also be wise to store your drink in glass—not in a plastic container—whenever possible. This is better than juicing, because you are eating the complete vegetable, including the fiber. The fiber is also known as a prebiotic, which is the "fertilizer" that "feeds" your gut flora. Your gut flora within your digestive tract is like a garden that needs to be maintained with fiber. The gut contains trillions of good bacteria that are critical for health and fighting many diseases. Furthermore, there are antioxidants and phytochemicals within these veggies that are unknown and are yet to be discovered that will be found to be beneficial to our bodies.

Cleaning a blender is easier than cleaning a juicer. Additionally, there is less wasted product, and less veggies are required to make this green drink. Moreover, you can add this to your daily goal of one to two pounds of veggies per day. Even if you make this green drink two or three times per week, you will enjoy the benefits. Drinking your veggies is just as good as eating them. They are broken down by the blender and are readily absorbed into your body for an immediate energy boost.

Just a quick word on two of the previously mentioned vegetables: kale and onions. They need to be pointed out because veggies are good, but these two are stellar in their nutritional advantages. For instance, kale is a very nutritionally dense veggie. The dark green color makes it rich in antioxidants and vitamin K. Dark leafy greens like kale are found in many longevity diets like the Mediterranean Diet and are consumed by many in the "Blue Zones."

Onions too are powerhouses that need to be incorporated into your diet in any way you can. They are part of a family of vegetation classified as allium which are leeks, garlic, chives, shallots, and scallions. Dr. Fuhrman cites them as roadblocks to gastric and prostate cancers. They are also powerful in fighting diabetes, with beneficial effects on the cardiovascular and immune systems as well.[28]

Fuhrman's GBOMBS + N

Dr. Joel Fuhrman has come up with a very helpful acronym to help us remember the critical foods we should consume daily. It so easy to adopt and adapt to your diet. All of these foods are whole foods—not processed—and are relatively inexpensive, and do not require much kitchen prep time nor clean-up! Easy and idiot-proof is the mantra here. One sees many recipes and dishes that are healthy, but require too much prep time and clean-up time! If it's not convenient, you will not want to stay with the protocol for very long; especially after a long day at work or school.

The GBOMBS + N:

G=Greens: all dark green leafy greens – spinach, kale, mustard and turnip greens

B=Beans: all varieties – red kidney, black, aduki, black-eyed pea, lentils, and cannellini beans

O=Onions: including leeks, garlic, chives, shallots, and scallions

M=Mushrooms (cooked): white, cremini, portobello, oyster, and shiitake

B=Berries: blueberries, strawberries, raspberries, and blackberries

S=Seeds: ground flaxseeds (stored in fridge), chia seeds, hemp seeds, and sesame seeds

N=Nuts (raw & unsalted): walnuts, almonds, and pecans

So What?

You say, what is the big deal with these GBOMBS+N? So glad you asked! In a TV interview with Dr. Pat Robertson on The 700 Club, Dr. Joel Fuhrman made a profound claim that should be of interest to young people, adults, and senior adults. He stated the following regarding beans: "Beans probably get a bad rap sometimes... I would say that eating beans is the hidden secret to longevity." Many people avoid beans sometimes due to gas. However, if one mixes it with small amounts of meat or other whole foods, that will not be an issue, and your body will adjust accordingly. For individuals with high blood sugar or type II diabetes, this one food will help them in a dramatic way. Beans lower the glycemic effect of all the foods we eat, stabilizing insulin levels and reducing inflammation, which is a leading factor in most diseases. No wonder all champions of longevity in the five "Blue Zones" eat—what? Beans!

Like it easy? Don't we all, with our busy schedules and fast-paced lifestyles. Well, here is a "fast food" that you can find in a can, organic and ready to eat—yes, beans. Many grocers now carry them that way. They do not have to be soaked or cooked. One can find organic beans ready to eat in a can; they are only pennies more, and you are assured of better quality without unwanted ingredients—just the beans. Some come with a flip top so that you do not even need a can opener. It is economical, fast, and idiot-proof! Feel free to jazz them up with your favorite seasonings and sauces, and to incorporate them with other foods. Spice is nice!

More good news—mushrooms inhibit cancer cell growth and promote cancer cell death, according to Dr. Fuhrman. They have a powerful role in preventing breast and prostate cancers. Raw mushrooms contain small amounts of a mild toxin called agaritine, which is greatly reduced in the cooking process.[29] Ladies and gentlemen, Dr. Fuhrman cites studies that women who consumed flaxseeds (must be ground for optimal absorption) and mushrooms regularly had a significant lower incident of breast cancer. Men had reduced rates of prostate cancer from these foods as well.[30]

Berries are classified as a superfood due to their rich antioxidant values and phytochemicals. Dr. Fuhrman states something that is very important to note: berries contain "flavonoids which affect gene expression and detoxification, inhibit cancer cell growth… and hinder inflammation."[31]

Convenience is king! Frozen berries are the king of convenience. One just takes out what one needs, then places the remainder back in the freezer. No waste, and a third of the cost of fresh berries—which are usually sprayed with fungicide to prevent spoilage. That is not the case with frozen berries which, through modern science, have been commercially washed and frozen quickly to retain the berries' freshness. For this reason, you can eat berries all year round and gain the same nutritional health benefit all year as well!

Nuts! They are a powerhouse of micronutrients that are extremely healthy to incorporate into your daily diet. As noted earlier, we are talking about raw and unsalted nuts, not processed nuts. They are convenient and make a great snack as well. No one gets fat eating these types of nuts. Why? Nuts naturally suppress your appetite, and they are a good heart and brain food loaded with omega-3 fatty acids, contain fiber to keep your colon healthy, and contain unsaturated fats. In short, they're all good!

Pat's Breakfast of Champions

A number of years ago, Pat Robertson shared with the viewers of *The 700 Club* a wonderful, healthy, and convenient breakfast that is loaded with good stuff. It is very simple to make—only a few minutes—and you are good to go and will be satisfied from hunger pangs for several hours.

It is basically oatmeal, with lots of other ingredients that make it so wonderful. It consists of old-fashioned oats, oat bran, blueberries, blackberries, raspberries, pecans, almonds, and walnuts. Sounds good—and tastes even better.

The author is sure that other price clubs sell the berries and nuts in bulk as Costco does. The writer just happens to use the brand that was featured on the broadcast. It showed the Kirkland brand for "Three Berry Blend," and Kirkland also sells large, separate bags of raw, unsalted almonds, walnuts, and pecans, which you should store in the fridge to retain freshness and to keep the nuts from becoming rancid. For an added nutritional punch, the author also adds organic wild (also known as low bush) frozen blueberries; they have double the antioxidant value of regular blueberries. They are smaller in size, but not flavor!

Putting it together: take out your frozen berries from the freezer the night before and put approximately one to two cups in a bowl and cover them with plastic wrap. Let them sit out on your counter overnight and they will be perfect the next morning to eat.

Just add about a third cup of old-fashioned oats and several tablespoons of oat bran on top of the berries. Then top with a small amount of all three nuts. The writer uses the center of his palm as a measure for each type of nut. You can adjust the amounts of the ingredients to your appetite and taste. It is important, however, to include all the ingredients to maximize the nutritional benefits of this breakfast.

Then just add your favorite milk: cow, rice, soy, or unsweetened almond milk. What's nice and convenient is the fact that the oatmeal does not have to be cooked. You can cook it if you do not like it right out of the box. But at least try it; I think you will be pleasantly surprised, and it is faster and easier!

A Dessert or Two
When I was growing up, my elementary teachers reminded us how to spell dessert and desert. Some things like that just seem to help you remember, and they stick with you. One of my third-grade teachers said repeatedly, "With dessert, which has two "s's," you always want two servings, unlike desert!" Well, touché—it works for me!

Two menu items the author would submit to you for your after-dinner enjoyment: dark chocolate and red wine. They complement each other very nicely. Dark chocolate contains polyphenols and flavanols that have powerful antioxidant activity. Dark chocolate also elevates your mood and lowers your blood pressure. It will satisfy your sweet tooth, and extend your life and enjoyment of the same! Choose at least 72 percent cacao or higher. The reason: the higher the percentage of cacao, the less sugar it contains—which is better, as we discussed earlier.

The second item to join the dark chocolate is red wine! It has been part of the Mediterranean lifestyle for centuries. Jesus thought it was good as well, when He performed His first miracle by turning water into wine! Jesus would not create something that is harmful or evil. And yes, there have been and will always be people who will abuse anything. The Bible is clear by calling such behavior folly and sin—the sin of drunkenness.[32]

Please do not forget your children and their desire for something sweet! Frozen grapes are a wonderful, convenient treat for them. They are rich in fiber and nutrients. Just make sure you buy organic grapes. Nonorganic grapes have pesticides and other unwanted chemicals.

Wash the grapes, dry them, and place them in the freezer on a tray. You will have a fun and tasty treat for the kids. You can also serve them a bowl of mixed berries with some raw macadamia nuts and walnuts.

Science confirms what we already know about the health benefits of red wine. Red, as opposed to white, has a greater antioxidant value. Dr. Gottfried states, regarding red wine: "If you do consume alcohol, red wine reduces mortality by more than 30 percent, according to a meta-analysis of sixteen studies." In fact, Dr. Gottfried suggests eliminating or severely limiting all alcohol but red wine.[33] This is wonderful to note: that our Lord has placed red wine on His earth for our enjoyment and health! This echoes what Scripture states: "Who richly provides us with everything for our enjoyment."[34]

Quality and quantity matter, in wine as in many areas of life. Organic wine is best, because conventional grapes are sprayed with pesticides which your body does not need.[35] Additionally, many additives are added to nonorganic wine that are not healthful.

Quantity matters. Too much of anything can turn the tide from a blessing to a bust! Wine is an adult beverage. The word *adult* is the operative word here. Meaning that it is reserved for responsible individuals. If you cannot drink it responsibly, by no means continue. If you have other issues that would affect your responsible use of wine, then choose to abstain. This is the "wonder and beauty" of being made in the image and likeness of God: we have the power of choice!

One six-ounce glass of red wine daily is the recommended amount.[36] This recommendation comes with all the advantages. It is the sweet spot, and with three squares of dark chocolate 72 percent or higher, you really are in a sweet spot of enjoyment and longevity!

Lifestyles That Boost Immunity

With the global pandemic of COVID-19, and with other viruses that enter populations at various times, it is imperative to boost our immune systems. Our Creator has designed us with a wonderful system that fights infections and viruses and heals the wounds that our bodies experience. Our God-given immune system functions as "soldiers" that are equipped to fight viruses, colds, and a multitude of diseases. Dr. David Perlmutter, neurologist and best-selling author of *Brain Wash*, which has been published in many languages, cites lifestyle choices that can greatly affect our immune system and our susceptibility to disease.

In an interview, Dr. Perlmutter cites specific and practical steps one can take to build one's soldiers to defend against COVID-19, viruses, and colds. He states, "The best thing is sleep. Sleep is incredibly undervalued and critically important to boosting the immune system. Even one night of nonrestorative sleep can significantly compromise the immune function that we so desperately depend on." The second item he cites is stress management. We have got to understand how critically damaging stress is on the immune system. We have all experienced being stressed out for one reason or another, then getting a bad cold.[37]

Dr. Perlmutter continues with simple things we can do to bolster our immune systems that can be gamechangers for our bodies and souls. Unlike so many, Dr. Perlmutter explains the close connection of the two for our immune function and overall wellbeing. He recommends having a good level of antioxidants like vitamin C on board, along with vitamin D and zinc. Moreover, he mentions that this is a time when we want to tap into the anti-inflammatory aspects of fish oil as well.[38]

Finally, Dr. Perlmutter summarizes simple things that Pat Robertson has talked about for a long time on The 700 Club. Dr. Perlmutter mentions things like getting a good night's sleep, engaging in physical exercise, eating a diet lower in sugar and lower in processed foods—and to that, we want to add prayer. Prayer has been shown to have an effect on the immune system, and that is absolutely our best friend as it relates to dealing with this viral infection.[39]

Truth is usually confirmed by more than

one witness. This is the case with Dr. Chauncey Crandall, who is a world-renowned cardiologist who has authored several books on faith, medicine, and heart disease. Interestingly, Dr. Crandall's protocols to prevent the COVID-19 virus are similar to the recommendations that Dr. Perlmutter espouses. In Dr. Crandall's book *Fight Back: Beat the Coronavirus*, he recommends simple things like exercise, enough sleep, lowering our stress, and eating correctly. He also makes the case for building up our immunity with things like vitamin C, vitamin D, vitamin A, zinc, selenium, garlic, and probiotics. All these items help us to develop a "shield," so that the COVID-19 virus cannot penetrate at the respiratory entry points, he explains.[40]

MOUTH MATTERS

◆ ◆ ◆

The writer was in the locker room at a health club and recently became friends with John, who competes in Iron Man competitions. He was a new father and was obviously excited about his baby girl, and he wanted to be the best and healthiest dad he could be. The writer was sharing that he had just finished reading Dr. Sara Gottfried's book, *Younger*, and that he had learned that simply flossing and brushing twice daily reduces one's mortality rate by 30 percent! John listened politely, and then the conversation was over. A week later the writer saw him again in the locker room, brushing his teeth at the sink. I commented, "That is a great thing to do for your health," to which he responded, "That is what you mentioned the other day, Doug." I forgot that I had mentioned

71

it to him, and most of all I was pleasantly surprised that he took it to heart and practice. That is wisdom in action!

And there is more: if you see the dentist only once per year, you raise your mortality risk to 30 to 50 percent as well.[41] As Dr. Gottfried states, "If you wonder how that works, it may interest you to know the following: you have more than seven hundred species of bacteria in your mouth."[42] This is a breeding ground for bacteria, and thus inflammation. The inflammation, starting in your mouth, begins its toxic travel through your body, setting in motion inflammation throughout your body and increasing your risk of many diseases and premature ageing.

Why is that? These bacteria are what account for "bad breath" and are the breeding ground for the beginning of this cascade of negative consequences to our bodies. Men may want to know that periodontal disease is more common in men than in women and is linked to early atherosclerosis and heart disease.[43] For this reason, please have your teeth cleaned twice per year by your dental professional.

The proper tools do make a difference, whatever the job entails. This is true with brushing our teeth as well. A power toothbrush is far superior and easier in getting the job done. They are not that expensive, and they are an investment that will reap rewards for you by lowering your dental bill due to reduced oral and dental issues!

EXERCISE
MEDICINE

◆ ◆ ◆

A re you feeling stressed out, depressed, fatigued, or maybe even fat and ugly? Well, I have a cheap prescription for you, with guaranteed results. Get moving—yes, I mean exercise!

We have become a very, very sedentary nation, and we have the butts to prove it! Besides the many health problems resulting from being too sedentary, our emotional health is weakened as well. Let's be frank: when you're out of shape, you feel crappy, and when you feel crappy, you are not enjoying the life you were meant to enjoy.

When you exercise you enjoy a whole host of benefits, such as: being able to better cope with stress; becoming less likely to get chronically depressed; enjoying a longer healthspan (which will give you more opportunities for rewards and crowns—heaven is not going to be the same for everyone);[44] looking better (younger); and having less fat to lug around!

The science of exercise gives good news! The data demonstrates what we all know intuitively. Namely, that physical activity—exercise—is good for your mental health and cognition, keeping your mind sharp! Dr. Ryan Olson, Assistant Professor, University of North Texas, found that endurance exercise reduced depressive symptoms by 58 percent.[45] In addition, Dr. Christiane Wrann, Assistant Professor of Medicine, Harvard Medical School, found that exercise results in the creation of new brain cells in the area of the brain concerned with the formation of new memories.[46]

LifeExtension provides an insightful observation into a physician's world and perspective. Patients come to physicians daily with complaints for which they do not want to take any active role to help themselves. Therefore, they are left to the only remedy that they can offer: to dispense a "magic" pill that will solve the problem without the patient changing their lifestyle.

LifeExtension has many physicians as part of their organization. They write, "Physicians often find it easier to prescribe a pill rather than to prescribe exercise, even though exercise may be more effective. Patients also often find that it is more convenient to take a pill than to exercise. Exercise is a medicine without the side effects of a drug. Too many people avoid experiencing the benefits of exercise at too great a cost."[47]

The medicine of exercise is always on sale, and if we avoid it, we will pay a harsh price. We can pay a little now, or pay a lot later, as one famous marketer said years ago! The word *medicine* is not an overstatement, since any physical activity is getting you in the right direction—and once moving, you can build on it.

Something as little as a brisk walk will get the job done. Just do it on a regular basis—no, not three times a month, but three to five times a week, with a friend if that enables you to be more disciplined. You can swim, bicycle, hike, jump rope, country or ballroom dance, join an aerobics class, or even do karate. Let it be fun! If it isn't fun, you will lose your passion and interest in a short period of time. At the same time, if you join some type of fitness club that offers fun activities that challenge you while you are acquiring a skill, you will feel mentally and physically refreshed. Moreover, you will meet other people of like passion and interest whom you will bless and who will bless you.

Exercise is as important as eating and sleeping—that is not an overstatement. We experience the immediate consequences of not eating with hunger pangs, and the immediate results of lack of sleep with crankiness, poor memory, and more. Yet lack of physical exercise also reaps very real consequences, though most times they are not immediate. Our physical bodies were designed for physical work or activity; when it does not happen the body atrophies, making it more prone to pathologies. The choices we make will have a cumulative effect on our bodies and temples

Cardio and Weights

The writer has been involved with fitness for years. He is a Sho-Dan (first master) in traditional Japanese karate. As such, he has observed that women and men many times focus on either cardio or weights, deleting either one to their detriment. It is not a case of "either/or" but of "both," as is said of many things in the wisdom of life.

Ladies first. We see women in fitness clubs many times doing cardio—which is of vital importance—yet neglecting weights. Weight bearing is especially important for women to maintain muscle mass and protect your skeletal system. Muscles protect your body and enable you to function more effectively, keeping your body's tone and form. Muscle burns more calories, allowing you to eat more foods that you enjoy.

Weights work for women. Weights place a load on your bones, which helps prevent osteoporosis which is common in women as they age. No worries, ladies—you will not get muscle-bound; rather, the weights will help you maintain the beauty and form your Master created you with and has given you the responsibility to maintain.

Men enjoy using weights, which is a good thing. They provide the same advantages that were cited above for women. Nonetheless, men have a weakness as well, and that is that they tend to overemphasize weights and neglect or minimize cardio. Getting "pumped," guys, includes raising your heart rate to strengthen your heart muscle, which needs exercise as well. We all need to be reminded about the basics at times; cardio for men is one of those basics we need to be reminded of.

Parents and Everybody Else
The world is a different place now, with many threats that were unthinkable years ago. Children are bullied and shot at by other children, and terrorist attacks make the news as well. Bad guys are always looking for prey, whether it be a child or even an unsuspecting adult.

Martial arts provide wonderful exercise for all ages, from young children to older adults.

There are many "dojos" (karate schools) everywhere that offer self-defense classes for people of all ages. Karate teaches one to be aware of their surroundings so that one can avoid many potentially dangerous situations.

Parents, do you want to protect your young children? Enroll them in a karate school that has what is called "pee-wee" classes. Any reputable karate school will also teach proper values like respect for authority, respect for others, and self-discipline, which is advantageous for all young minds and hearts. They will not turn out to be violent troublemakers. Rather, quite the opposite. There is something that happens to a trained child or adult who knows how to defend themselves that gives them a quiet confidence, with nothing to prove. Furthermore, bullies and bad guys instinctively know by the look and demeanor that this person is not a lamb; he will look for other, easier prey.

Parents, as your children earn belts and go up in rank, they will have a sense of earned pride and satisfaction. The author knows a father that has both his daughter and son enrolled in a taekwondo school for kids. Both son and daughter have achieved several belts already. The father shared with me that it has been a wonderful tool to teach them obedience within the family; just the threat of taking away their rank causes a sudden change of attitude!

Ladies, you are invited as well, no matter what age. One of the author's favorite stories that he watched on *The 700 Club* many years ago was about a grandmother. She was involved in street ministry in an urban area, doing what the Lord had called her to do—preaching the gospel to anyone who would listen on the street. People knew her as she was a familiar face on the street, doing good.

One day, a would-be mugger attempted to rob this grandmother, who "happened" (in Bible terms, we call this divine providence) to be a black belt in karate. Well, the bad guy got more than he bargained for as she quickly and appropriately dispatched him! The moral of the story is that learning how to defend oneself is wise and keeps you fit for life.

The Power of Fish Oil

◆ ◆ ◆

Everyone seemingly knows that fish oil is beneficial to one's health. Yet the benefit is more than what people imagine; that is not a hyperbolic statement. It is beneficial from cradle to grave, as you will see, and our Maker has placed it in our world to combat disease and make us thrive.

There is a considerable body of medical evidence demonstrating the profound effect of the omega-3 fatty acids found in fish oil, and how they combat disorders and disease. It is true that there are omega-3s found in avocados, nuts, seeds, brussels sprouts, and other sources as well. Nonetheless, fish oil is one of the most potent sources of this powerful anti-inflammatory wonder. In one large study, those whose values (omega-3 blood levels) were among the top 20 percent had a 34 percent lower risk of death from any cause. It lowers one's risk of cardiovascular disease by 39 percent, and gives one a 42 percent lower risk of coronary heart disease and a 55 percent lower risk of stroke.[48] This is wonderful news, and it gets even better on chronic illnesses that make so many miserable.

Let us look at just a sample of some disorders and diseases that omega-3s can change in a powerful way: cholesterol management, cognitive decline, anxiety and depression, diabetes, enhanced immune system, eye health, hypertension, osteoarthritis, breast and prostate cancer, rheumatoid arthritis, skin aging, asthma, and even acne.[49] Again, this is just a small sample of the many diseases and disorders that have inflammation as the culprit of these maladies. Omega-3s' anti-inflammatory properties interfere and arrest the inflammatory response that these aliments ignite. They are the providential "fire extinguishers" that are critical to our health and enjoyment of life!

Cradle to Grave: Get the Word Out!

The cardiac benefits of omega-3s in fish oils are well-known and documented. This is part of the reason why we see the widespread use of fish oil. However, according to Dr. Julius Goepp, less known and equally important is the benefit to brain health. Dr. Goepp states, "Their (omega-3s) paramount role is optimizing many facets of brain function, from depression, cognition, and memory, to mental health."[50] Dr. Goepp continues to make the case of why this nutrient is so critical to our brain health when he continues, "Recent research has opened up a new horizon in our understanding of omega-3s' profound ability to halt age-related decline and pathology, shattering the long-held medical belief that brain shrinkage and nerve cell death is progressive and irreversible."[51] This is wonderful news that should be shouted from the rooftops!

Dr. Daniel Amen, a psychiatrist and New York Times best-selling author, echoes the critical importance of omega-3s as well. In his book *Healing On the Inside*, he outlines the benefits of omega-3s to unlock your brain's healing potential to overcome anxiety, anger, stress, and trauma. Dr. Amen even states that "everybody should be taking omega-3s every day." We have a crisis in this country of low levels of omega-3s. He then asks the question: "Why should you care?" Then Dr. Amen answers his own question: "Well, 25 percent of your brain is actually made up of omega-3s, so if you're low, you are not thinking right."[52]

Future Moms and Pregnant Moms
Omega-3 fatty acids are critical even before the cradle, as was demonstrated in the prestigious journal Lancet, as Dr. Goepp cites: "In one of the largest studies of its kind, scientists analyzing the diets of 12,000 pregnant women found that children of those who consumed the least omega-3s were 48 percent more likely to score in the lowest quartile on IQ tests."[53]

Quantity Matters!
Why the quantity matters is due to the make-up of our brains. Along with most organs and

parts of our body they must be fed the proper nutrients, otherwise they starve and operate at subpar levels. Dr. Goepp explains why the brain needs to be fed omega-3s when he states, "Approximately 8 percent of the brain's matter is comprised of omega-3 fatty acids."[54] He continues by describing how docosahexaenoic acid (DHA) and eicosapentaenoic acid (EPA) play vital roles in protecting our brains from oxidative damage, inflammation, and the cumulative destruction inflicted by chronic insults.[55]

This leads us to the question: "How much fish oil should I take?" This question is critical, because various brands have different amounts of DHA and EPA—the nutrients that comprise omega-3s. Consequently, one needs to look at the back of the bottle, where the amounts of DHA and EPA are listed separately. The manufacturer will have a suggested dose of one or two softgels. The one the writer picked up from a grocer to use as an example recommends taking one softgel containing 1,000 mgs of fish oil. However, when one looks at the EPA amount, it is only 180 mg and DHA is only 120 mg. These are grossly inadequate amounts of EPA and DHA, according to the latest research.

The co-founder of LifeExtension Buyers Club, William Faloon, addressed this critical issue that most health professionals miss. Almost everyone knows that fish oil is beneficial, and most people take it daily. However, most do not take adequate amounts of fish oil to obtain the critical levels of DHA and EPA that maintains adequate blood levels to feed the brain, promote and protect cardiovascular health, fight premature aging, and combat many pathologies, as cited earlier.

Target Range: 1400 mg EPA and 1000 mg DHA

The numbers matter for gray matter! These are the targeted amounts of omega-3s that adults should take daily. LifeExtension and their team of many research MDs and PhDs demonstrated that these are the optimal amounts of DHA and EPA for most people to reach proper blood levels of omega-3s.[56] Using the example of fish oil mentioned earlier, one would have to take approximately eight softgels of that brand to reach targeted levels of omega-3s. The math is straightforward; given the EPA of 180 and the 120 DHA on the back of the label, one would need to take approximately eight softgels with this brand to get to the targeted range of 1400 EPA and 1000 DHA.

Quality does matter with fish oil, as with most things in life. It is only pennies more weekly to purchase a quality fish oil that you are placing in your body and the temple of the living Lord. You are certainly worth the nominal extra cost to obtain wonderful benefits to your cardiovascular health, brain and nerve health, vision health, and joint health!

The gold standard for fish oil is to procure one that is "IFOS" certified. IFOS stands for International Fish Oil Society. IFOS checks for heavy metals (toxins), the actual amount of omega-3s, levels of oxidation, and other critical indices that measure the manufacturer's claims. They are an independent laboratory that is performing these tests for the consumers' benefit.

The writer has placed two different man-ufacturers in the end notes that have received a five-star rating from IFOS. Moreover, and equally importantly, both brands contain the correct amounts of EPA (1400 mg) and DHA (1000 mg), when one takes their recommended dosage. As always, please follow the directions on the label.[57]

Omega-3 Index Complete

The quantities given for EPA and DHA may seem high to some—even to some health care providers who are unaware that there is now a commercial blood test that is available to everyone to check one's blood levels of ome-ga-3s. Unfortunately, most health care provid-ers will not include this in your lab work unless you ask for it. Remember: "Healthcare is self-care."

The omega-3 index blood test will help you know exactly your EPA and DHA levels. The target range for your EPA and DHA blood levels is between 8 percent and 12 percent for optimal health. A few years ago it was not available; now it is available at most labs and drawing stations.[58]

As with any supplement, please check with your health care professional before taking.

Children: Smarty-Pants and Super-Brainy

Moms and Dads, please do not forget your children with their hungry little minds! Their young and developing minds need these essential fatty acids to develop to their God-ordained potential. This can be obtained through their diet and/or supplementation. There are many foods that contain omega-3s, such as raw nuts, seeds (ground flax seeds & chia seeds), eggs, avocados, brussels sprouts, and wild-caught salmon, to mention a few. However, if you have a challenging time trying to get your little ones to eat these omega-3 foods, you may want to supplement as well.

Here are two different sources that one can utilize. They specialize in age-appropriate doses of omega-3s for your future little "Einsteins": Smarty-Pants by Toddler Complete, and Super-Brainy by Olly.[59] Both products offer a rich source of omega-3s, and your little ones will readily eat them. Why? They are in gummy form! As always, please check with your child's pediatrician when giving any supplement to your child.

Section Two:
The Soul

Jesus: "What good will it be for someone to gain the whole world, yet forfeit their soul?"[60]

5 Rs to Freedom in Your Thought Life

◆ ◆ ◆

Most of our difficulties begin in our minds. What we think about has consequences to our well-being, our physical health, and our eternal soul. Most people would agree with that statement. However, that fact does not address that many times we develop strongholds or destructive thinking patterns that keep us locked into a "holding pattern," like a jet that has to circle in the sky, waiting for clearance from air-traffic control before it can make a safe landing. We have an enemy of our souls who wants to rob us of the joy of living and keep us in these holding patterns that sap our emotional strength and vitality for life, and our enjoyment of the fullness of life that the Master promises for all. Most of us are unaware that there is a spiritual conflict (an unseen war) that is taking place, that is unseen yet has real consequences in the physical world in which we live. C.S. Lewis said it best when he stated, "We live in enemy-occupied territory."[61] Professor Lewis's statement is affirmed in the Bible: "Dear friends, I urge you, as foreigners and exiles, to abstain from sinful desires, which wage war against your soul."[62]

In his book *Healing On the Inside*, Jon Eargle[63] has developed a simple protocol to combat the "recording" that many times we let play over and over, which keeps our minds trapped in a destructive cycle of defeated thinking. The Bible gives us a plan to execute when we engage in spiritual warfare against a very real devil, who has been using our minds for centuries as a gateway to gain a stronghold in our thinking that leads to sinful attitudes and behaviors that we "think" we cannot shake free of, for many reasons.

The writer discovered this foundational skill set for freedom and peace in our minds one Sunday afternoon while listening to a broadcast called "Totally Transformed," hosted by Dr. Connie Borden. "Dr. Connie," as she refers to herself on-air, has a doctorate from Regent University and has been in practice as a clinical psychologist for many years. The title of her book is *Saved, But Not Free* by Dr. Connie Borden. The title contains the dilemma that many Christians find themselves in today—not free, and bound up in this woundedness and in a cycle of negative attitudes and patterns of behavior. It showcases that many of us living our Christian lives today are needlessly defeated, and tells us how to break free of these self-destructive patterns where the enemy of our soul wants us to stay trapped due to ignorance. "Dr. Connie" has modified and developed these five "Rs" with years of clinical experience and many true stories that have led to freedom. Her ministry is called www.totallytransformed.org, which is a great resource for further help to enjoy the freedom that our Lord promises to those who seek it.

We are active participants in this process. So many believers are passive in their faith walk, not understanding that we have a role to "work out our salvation," not work for our salvation. For this reason, the New Testament is replete with imperatives for us to implement. Our Creator has made us free moral agents with the capacity to choose to love and follow Him, unlike robots! He has given us the personal power of choice, which sets us apart in His glorious creation

"Dr. Connie" said something that was a game-changer for anyone, or for couples who are struggling in their relationships. In the broadcast she was relating stories (anonymously) of individuals and couples that had come to see her for counseling for issues that were keeping them in various attitudes and actions that were contrary to the abundant life that Jesus promises. After hearing their stories, with the common theme of the woundedness that we are all subject to in a fallen and broken world, she would introduce them to the strategy of the five "Rs" for freedom in their thought life. Then she told how many individuals and couples who had faithfully adopted this protocol for dealing with these issues, which had become strongholds in their thinking and emotions, had no further need of counseling! The power of the weapons that our Master has given us are mighty and effective. Yet unfortunately, many people do not know what to do, nor that there is a real devil who has a plan for their lives just like Jesus has a plan for their lives! The two are worlds apart: Satan's plan is to steal, kill, and destroy. The Master's plan is that we may live life to the full![64]

Recognize and Reject the Wrong Thoughts! Have you ever found yourself sitting in church, driving your car, grocery shopping, or just hanging out, when out of nowhere you get this bitter, lustful, or destructive thought that seemingly just "pops into your mind"? Satan is real, and so are his angels, called demons. He is like a monkey in a banana tree that is jumping around, wanting to plant thoughts that are contrary to the truth. Satan and his demons have a "corporate mission statement" that he has posted in his conference room. The mission: "steal, kill, and destroy."[65] The devil and his demons cannot read your mind; however, they have been observing mankind for millennia, so they know what buttons to push on you and me. One of his basic weapons is to cast doubt on the goodness of God and His Word. Adam and Eve took the bait and got caught, and the devil is still running the same effective playbook with the unsuspecting and uninformed. Many of us are also forgetful of the power and armor of the Lord, which He has given to all His disciples who appropriate His divine weapons!

The first "R" for having freedom in your thought life is to "recognize and reject" thoughts that are contrary to revealed truth! When we are going about the business of life, and a thought that is contrary to the revealed Word of God pops up, we must take it prisoner or captive. When (not if) the sinful thought comes, we must recognize it and reject it, not based on feelings or emotions. The devil sows a destructive thought, and if we are not careful, we believe another lie—that we cannot control what we think about. That is a lie from the hallways of hell. We have the power of choice, and we have the power to choose what we think about.

This is made clear in Scripture, which does not lie and is battle-tested, working every time when implemented by all of God's kids! When the destructive, enticing thoughts begin playing their recordings in our minds, we need to activate the delivering power of the Word, which states: "We demolish arguments and every pretension that sets itself up against the knowledge of God, and we take captive every thought to make it obedient to Christ."[66] This is the first and primary step of the 5 Rs: to recognize and reject any thought that is not in agreement with the Master of our souls.

One learns to recognize and reject what is contrary to Christ as one reads and mediates on His Word. Hearing and feeding your soul— which includes your mind, will, and emotions—with the living words of Jesus gives you discernment in recognizing deception and the subtle lies of the devil. For example, you may be going about your business and all of a sudden, a thought just "pops" into your head, thinking about what your friend said to you on social media; you addressed the issue and forgave her, yet an unforgiving and a bitter spirit begins to play in your mind. Likewise, maybe you have been under stress at work and suddenly you feel the urge to look at porn after repenting several years earlier. The thoughts are becoming more frequent, and you feel the weight and heat of the temptation. Both individuals have recognized and chosen to reject these thoughts, which leads to the second step which breaks the power of those seductive suggestions of Satan.

Rebuke That (Evil) Spirit in the Mighty Name of Jesus
As we stated earlier, evil spirits are real! Both Jon Eargle and Dr. Connie observe that evil spirits are simply Satan's army for use against his enemy—the people of God. They feed on negative emotions such as past wounds, infecting them and making them worse. The evil spirits are trying to infect and pick at the wounds to thwart the healing ministry of Jesus that is ongoing.

One can usually identify the spirit by what you are thinking or feeling: anger, depression, unbelief, rage, lust, and loneliness, to mention a few. All of these thoughts, negative or evil, are common to everyone at one time or another; yes, even to your pastor or any other godly man or woman you may know. The Bible is very clear in that all temptations are common to all men and all women.[67] The problem is not the thought itself, but what we do with it that can be destructive.

This is where we have power in Christ to break the chain of lies that are played over and over in our minds. As believers in Christ, we have His mighty power![68] This power in the Lord gives us authority over these unseen but real spirits.[69] The Bible tells us through the apostle Paul: "For though we live in the world, we do not wage war as the world does. The weapons we fight with are not the weapons of the world. On the contrary, they have divine power to demolish strongholds."[70] It is a bold statement that is emboldened because Jesus lives in you, and He has given you authority when you call on Him!

When we recognize and reject the wrong thoughts and rebuke them in the power of Jesus, they must go, as promised by the Lord! This does not just happen in a passive manner, however. We must actively engage the enemy (Satan) by recognizing and rejecting and then rebuking him in the name of the King of the universe—Jesus Himself!

Recite What God's Word Says and Renew Your Mind in It

As both authors (Mr. Eargle and Dr. Connie) emphasize, the world we live in is constantly bombarding us with its message, which is contrary to the revealed will of God. What is the revealed will of God? It is not complicated nor hidden, but is given to us in His eternal and established Word. Unlike any other written word, His Word is living and active, and is depicted intentionally as a sword that is an offensive weapon, that destroys false beliefs we have about ourselves and our circumstances. Consequently, we must view our lives from God's perspective, not the world's perspective.

Master the Master! Do what Jesus did when He was confronted by the "father of lies" to take a path contrary to the one given to Him by His Father. Jesus recited the living Word when challenged to doubt the goodness and faithfulness of the Father. Jesus said: "It stands written, men [and women] do not live on bread alone, but on every word that comes from the mouth of God."[71] Please do not miss this fact that can transform your life in ways that you cannot fully imagine now: if Jesus recited the living Word of God, how much more should we! Again, master the Master; He said it out loud to activate its power, as we should. The Word of God pierces the powers of the demonic world and transforms the atmosphere where we find ourselves.

Not only does declaring the Word out loud change the atmosphere, it has the power to change us and our thought life. The Bible tells us that the secret is to think in the way that He designed us to think—not trapped in the chain of thoughts that are self-destructive and that produce the fruit of misery to our body, mind, and soul. The Scripture states: "Do not conform to the pattern of this world, but be transformed by the renewing of your mind. Then you will be able to test and approve what God's will is—His good, pleasing and perfect will."[72] The power point from that Word is that the spoken Word has the ability to transform and renew our minds, which is an awesome promise to lay hold of for all followers of Christ.

Resist the Devil

To complete the thought of resistance, it comes with a promise. Namely, resist the devil, and he will flee. We are not told to run, but to take our stand and resist—and God, who cannot lie, states that he (the devil) will flee. There is, however, a positive action that we are told to enact before we resist the devil.

The half-brother of our Lord, James, under the divine inspiration of God the Holy Spirit, said this: "Submit yourselves, then, to God" (James 4:7 NIV).

The Word enjoins us to line ourselves up

with God's will for our lives. What is God's will, you may ask? It is stated clearly for us in the Bible. What is the one nine-letter word that can sum up most of the sixty-six books of the Bible, and spells love for our Lord and promised blessing from Him? Obedience. As we choose to submit to His wonderful will for our lives and resist the devil's lies, God gives us His Word that the devil must yield the right of way.[73]

Rejoice in All Things

The Bible tells us, "Rejoice always, pray continually, give thanks in all circumstances; for this is God's will for you in Christ Jesus."[74] It is interesting to note that God does not tells us to do these things if we "feel" like rejoicing, praying, and giving thanks. Many times, our feelings are fickle and feckless. The apostle Paul does not tell us to be thankful and rejoice "for" our adversities in life. Rather, Scripture teaches us that the Lord wants us to be thankful and rejoice "in" our difficulties. There is a rainbow that shines during these dark, cloudy times when we offer up, out of obedience, the sacrifice of praise. We experience the real and transcendent presence of our living Lord!

It is important to note that "rejoice," "pray," and "give thanks" are all imperatives in the Greek. The Father always honors obedience to His Word. We can expect positive consequences when we obey Him in child-like faith. A young child does not always understand why the parents expect certain behaviors or allow trying circumstances, but the young child trusts the goodness of their parents. Those of you who are parents understand this readily. You are pleased to reward your children when they obey you. Why are you pleased when they obey? Because you are made in the Father's image; you are pleased with obedience in your children, just as He is pleased when we obey Him as well. We reflect His nature.

Praise is a weapon when we are in a battle of any kind. The Psalmist gives us a glimpse into why praise and worship of our Maker is vital to breakthrough in our lives. David states that "Through the praise of children and infants you have established a stronghold against your enemies, to silence the foe and the avenger"[75] Satan desires to be worshipped and followed due to his hubris; he is jealous of the Father, Jesus, and God the Holy Spirit. When we praise our Lord, Satan leaves, because he is not being praised nor worshipped.

David continues the positives of praise when He states that the Lord rests upon or is enthroned upon the praises of His people.[76] This is counter-intuitive to most of us. When we are overwhelmed by difficulties, like a loss of some kind, we do not feel like giving praise and thanks to our Lord. Nonetheless, this is the secret to happiness that will amaze you every time. When we start giving thanks to God— not for the tragedies, but during our trials—the demonic spirits must flee. Chains and strongholds are broken through praise and worship, not complaining. As has been said, "When we complain, we remain; when we praise, we are raised"!

This is pictured for us so well in the true story of two men the author recently read about. They were not US citizens and did not enjoy the privileges and protections that we enjoy in the United States. They were doing missionary work for the Lord, living obediently to the Word of God.

While engaged in their ministry, some people got very upset with the two men, so they seized them physically and forcibly took them before a local judge. False testimony was given against them. No defense attorney was assigned to them, so they were sentenced by the same judge to be beaten severely and then thrown in jail. Furthermore, the judge was so hostile to these men, he told the jailer to put their feet in "stocks" and in the most secure part of the prison.

This prison was not like ours in the United States: no climate control, no TVs, no gym to work out and lift weights in, and no electric lights, so it was pitch black. Rats were prevalent, and the stench of other prisoners who had not bathed for a long period of time, along with human waste, was pungent!

Late that night, the older of the two men said to the younger man, "We need to worship

God now." But the younger man said, "My back is raw, and these stocks are hurting my feet... I really don't feel like praising God right now—look where we are!" But the elder brother encouraged him: "We must praise our Lord! We need to start giving Him thanks. Let's sing some hymns to God!" Not only did they begin singing and praising God, but they did it loudly—so loudly that the other prisoners heard them as well. As a matter of fact, the other prisoners were listening intently!

During all this praise, there was a prison break! This prison break, however, was not man-made, but a heavenly earthquake. Yes, you got it—the Lord of all creation gave the order in response to two men who knew that they should always be worshipping, no matter what. And, yes, the Lord gave the order and all the prison doors opened, and all the chains of all the prisoners came loose! Yes, you guessed it, this is the true story of Paul and Silas—beaten, imprisoned, and in stocks in the Bible, in Acts 16!

Tertullian, an early church father, born to

a Roman centurion, converted to Christianity in AD 145, just a few years after this event. He stated a truth we all need to embrace and practice: "The legs feel nothing in the stocks when the heart is in heaven." Tertullian is reminding us that when we feel our lives are in the "stocks" of difficulties, disappointments, and devastation, we need to raise our voices in thanks, songs, and praises to heaven. Again, praise is a weapon!

Saint Paul said this a second time when he was imprisoned in Philippi, "Whatever you have learned or received or heard from me, or seen in me—put it into practice."[77] Paul is commanding us to "Do what I do" and "Do what I did"!

When we begin to praise the Lord during spiritual battles, divine power is unleashed, and our strongholds and chains are broken. Jesus shows no favoritism; what He did for Paul and Silas, He will always do for each man, woman, boy, and girl today. What most of us do not understand—and it is the reason we do not see the same miraculous activity today—is that it takes faith to worship and praise God during these times of adversity. We are told to "offer up a sacrifice of praise."[78] What Jesus has done for others, He will do for you. Jesus is the same… He does not change.[79]

VOICE ACTIVATE GOD'S POWER

◆ ◆ ◆

Some segments of the church understand this, and some abuse it, but most do not understand and therefore are missing out on the full gospel of Jesus Christ. The writer is making a point to say the "full" gospel of Jesus. The Greek word *euaggelion*, "gospel," literally means "good news." Many times we are hesitant to share this good news, because we forget what it was like to have our sins forgiven, having been delivered from strongholds in our lives and healed from our diseases. We have been divinely selected by the Son of God to communicate all this "good news" that He has made known!

Many Christians believe that they are saved and on their way to heaven in the future, and that is where the gospel ends for them. In some parts of the church, some words and teachings of Jesus are noticeably avoided—to our detriment, unfortunately. Jesus chose His words carefully, because words matter; they always have and always will. For this reason, we need to heed all the words of the Master; if we avoid or neglect some of the words of Jesus, we do so at our own peril and miss out on the full measure of life He wants for us, now and in heaven as well! Heaven will not be the same for everyone; I shall explain and validate that most important fact later.

It has been very in vogue in the church and in secular circles to hear the statement "The truth will set you free." The writer calls this "bumper-sticker Christianity." Many people want to condense all of Jesus' statements down to one simple slogan. Many times because they do not want to nor are they willing to study His Word as we are commanded.[80] When believers stand before Jesus at the award ceremony for each believer, some are going to suffer loss because of their willful ignorance of His Word. Jesus will be saying to them at the judgment seat, "This is what you could have received if you had known and obeyed My Word."

When we master the Master, we do as Jesus did and enjoy the results that Jesus enjoyed. This is portrayed vividly for us when Jesus the God/man was led into the desert and was tempted by the enemy of our souls: the devil. Jesus the God/man felt hunger and was enticed by the tempter to turn stones into bread. Jesus did not debate or argue with the devil; rather, Jesus declared out loud God's holy and eternal Word. Jesus said: "It stands written: 'Man does not live on bread alone, but on every word that comes from the mouth of God.'"[81]

The power point for us is that the spoken Word of God drives the enemy out of our lives and more! The spoken Word actually changes the atmosphere of our lives, as Jesus promised when He stated: "Truly I tell you" (this introduction is a solemn declaration that He is making to get our attention), "if anyone says to this mountain, 'Go, throw yourself into the sea,' and does not doubt in their heart but believes that what they say will happen, it will be done for them."[82]

Jesus declared out loud to the devil—and the unseen spirit world—God's eternal Word. If we place our active faith in God's living Word, miraculous things happen. The author of Hebrews states: "The word of God is alive and active."[83] We are to put our faith (which is active, and not passive) in God's Word. Jesus cannot lie, as He states in His Word![84]

Many years ago, the writer was sparring in karate—not kumite, just light sparring. No need for a mouthpiece, or so he thought. Well, the one time the writer did not have his mouthpiece, he got punched in the mouth—and of course, loosened his front tooth. Consequently, he went to the dentist and needed a crown. However, the enemy is always at work, trying to discourage God's children through adversities big and small. Unfortunately, the crown did not do the job, and the author had to go back several more times for oral surgery due to infection. He remembers the third time, when the dentist left him alone in the dental chair for a few minutes. He began to feel sorry for himself; this was going very badly, his girlfriend had just broken off a serious relationship, his job as a computer operator while in seminary was being phased out, and his dental insurance was therefore being terminated. He began to cry in the chair; the feeling of fear began to grip him and overwhelmed him. Although he was in seminary at the time, as mentioned, he did not understand how to activate God's Word in his life.

Fast forward about twenty years. He went to the dentist for a routine check, and the dentist observed that there was some decay near the crown of that same tooth and the crown would have to be replaced. No big deal—so he thought, until he noticed that the dentist was pressing very hard on the tooth, and it became loose. Later the dentist said, "It's probably infected, and you need an implant."

He went home that day and said to himself, "I am not going to let fear grip me again—like it did years ago—over this! No, God is faithful, and He has never failed me when I hold Him to His Word!" In the next day or two, he and his wife were watching *The 700 Club* (CBN), as usual, for a Christian perspective on the news. Well, for whatever reason (divine providence), we watched the segment with Pat Robertson and co-host Terry Meeuwsen where they would have "words of knowledge" regarding people who would be healed. Then Pat began to describe a man who had an infection that was in the upper area of his mouth above his tooth: "Not the tooth itself, but the problem is above it." My wife looked at me, shocked—and yes, we both realized God the Holy Spirit had used Pat to describe my condition exactly.

The writer felt nothing—no warm sensation or feeling of "electricity" in that area. Yet he knew that God the Holy Spirit had spoken through His servant Pat Robertson. The author believed by faith in the proclaimed Word that he was healed. He made an appointment with an oral surgeon, and the x-ray confirmed what he knew already. No infection was shown on the picture; he was healed! Later the writer went to another dentist and relayed the story to him. This new dentist commented that the tooth with the issue was stronger and did not move at all compared to the one next to it! What is interesting to note is that sometimes God leaves us reminders of His healing work; he can still feel the same feeling in that tooth, but it is firm in its foundation. A reminder that we do not live by our feelings, but on the fact of God's eternal Word.

God's Word must be declared aloud in our lives. God asks a question to us regarding His Word: "Is not my word like fire... and like a hammer that breaks a rock in pieces?" (Jeremiah 23:29 NIV). Jesus is looking for a few men, women, boys, and girls who will be like Elijah, calling down fire from heaven on the territories the devil wants to take and smashing his evil works with the hammer of heaven—God's eternal Word declared in faith! The prophet declared that God's Word has power like fire and a hammer, that can consume and break any obstacle we encounter this side of heaven![85]

King Solomon echoes Jesus' later words as well. Solomon tells us the power of our confession when he states, "Death and life are in the power of the tongue, and those who love its use will eat its fruit."[86] We are enjoined to declare out loud God's promises over ourselves, our spouses, our children, our health, our education, our safety, our careers, our ministries, and our futures. Whatever the circumstances that challenge us and make us anxious, we need only to go to the treasure chest of promises and find the ones needed and declare them over our lives. The resounding theme throughout every book and story in the Bible is that God always honors the individual who has faith in His Word!

Protection in the Last Days of Pestilence

Jesus was clear that no one will know the day or hour of His return, but the "signs" can be seen by the discerning. In Luke 21, one of the signs that Jesus describes that the end is near is that "There will be... pestilences in various places, and fearful events."[87]

The power of God's Word is not changed nor diminished by any global pandemic, including the COVID-19 virus and similar viruses. The Bible is replete with many promises of protection for such a time as this. Psalm 91 is one of these promises that is activated by the declaration of faith in His stated promise of protection. The complete Psalm is filled with various dangerous situations that arise that the recipients can be delivered from. This happens when they combine two things: they combine "declaration" with "faith." In verse two (NIV) it states, "I will say of the LORD, 'He is my refuge and my fortress, my God, in whom I trust.'"

The LORD expands His promises further in verse 14 (NIV). The LORD says, "'Because he loves me,' says the LORD, 'I will rescue him; I will protect him, for he acknowledges my name.'" Most of us overthink this promise and many promises like this, rather than just simply taking God at His Word with child-like faith. When we declare God's Word, fear will flee, and our inner man will be fortified as we activate Psalm 91 in our lives!

A SABBATH REST

◆ ◆ ◆

The title of this chapter states the lifestyle point that is important: namely, that we all need a Sabbath rest. We are molded and modeled after our Creator. God ceased from all His activity after six days and rested. It is obvious that God does not require physical rest as we do. Yet He set a pattern for us to follow that is beneficial for us physically, emotionally, and spiritually.

Many of the "Blue Zones" groups we previously mentioned practice taking a Sabbath rest from their work and daily duties. Dan Buettner, the author of *The Blue Zones*, spent a Sabbath with the Seventh Day Adventist in Loma Linda, California. Buettner referred to the Sabbath that they took as a "sanctuary in time." That is a beautiful word picture he makes that we all need to enjoy.

Randy Roberts, the pastor of Loma Linda University Church, told Dan Buettner about the spirit of the Sabbath and why he thinks it helps people live longer: "I've heard repeatedly from students in rigorous programs like medicine and dentistry, and from faculty too, that they can't wait for the Sabbath to come because they have a guilt-free time when they don't have to study or do some other obligation. They can just be with their family and friends and with God, and just relax and rejuvenate."[88]

Pastor Roberts said it well. With all the time-saving devices that we have, most people would agree that they have less time to accomplish all of their given responsibilities. Chronic stress is a foe to our body and soul. Chronic stress causes us to age prematurely; it also breaks down the door of our body's defenses against disease. So too the soul. The soul, which makes you "you," is wrapped in a body and gets empty and dry when not given a "sanctuary of time." When we do not take "soul rest," we are prone to the maladies of our world: depression, anxiety, meaninglessness, and a lack of peace and fulfillment. Personal peace and fulfillment can only be filled by the One who made us and who gives us His peace.[89]

One of the greatest kings in history was king David. David's kingdom is mentioned throughout the Bible. David had many responsibilities that included leading the military, political administration, and spiritual leadership for the nation of Israel, as well as a large family. In the entire Bible, there is only one man of whom the LORD of all creation says, "David... [is] a man after My own heart."[90] There is no praise or prize that any woman or man could give on this earth that would rival a commendation such as was given to David!

David was a very busy man, as noted. Nonetheless, with all his duties, it is repeated over and over that David was a worshipper of God. David sang and played his musical instrument before the Lord, in private and public worship. Interestingly, David partnered with God the Holy Spirit in writing many of the Psalms.

Our Maker tells us to turn it off one day per week and enjoy a sanctuary of peace and rest. We can do this when we realize and trust that He is working through us with what needs to be accomplished each day. In contrast, when we falsely think that it is solely us working alone, performing the assignments of our lives, it places a burden that gets heavy over time. Our Lord wants to partner with us in all the activities we engage in, secular or sacred; for there is no such distinction made by Him! Our divine Designer has told us, "Whatever you do, do it all for the glory of God."[91] Meaning, whatever we do—make God look good!

As the writer has said earlier, master the Master. Jesus observed the weekly Sabbath, as was His custom. He spent time with His heavenly Father, His disciples, in the synagogue, and resting. Moreover, Jesus spent regular times early in the morning as the gospels indicate, getting alone in worship and spending time with His Father.

If Jesus, as Lord and Son of God, felt it necessary to take a weekly "sanctuary in time" and spend daily time worshipping, listening, and talking with His Father—how about you and me? We are blessed not for knowing but for doing what the Master did. In our western culture, we equate belief with knowledge. Jesus was making a radical truth claim that one only knows something when one acts on and practices what he or she professes to know. In the economy of the kingdom of God (His kingdom is filled with principles for activating power and blessings), Jesus teaches that we only know and are blessed when we practice His teachings. Talking to His followers, He enjoins them: "Now that you know these things, you will be blessed if you do them."[92] The realized blessing that Jesus is holding forth to His followers is conditional: "... if you do them."

The weekly Sabbath or "sanctuary of rest" becomes a lifestyle when we practice it daily as the first order of the day. When we open our eyes in the morning we should begin talking (praying) to the Lord, telling Him that we love Him and thanking Him for loving us. You say that your mind begins to get flooded with the many duties and concerns that are on your plate. This is why it is imperative that we go to Him first as our Source for wisdom, peace, love, and favor, to partner with Him as He accomplishes His plans through us that day. Even if you spend only a few minutes with the Lord, you will begin to cherish your time with Him more and more. This will steel the spine of your soul, making you a ready soldier, equipped for every task set before you for the day.

Communion with God was the first daily practice of Jesus and of David. The Bible states: "Very early in the morning, while it was still dark, Jesus got up, left the house and went off to a solitary place, where He prayed."[93] David too had the same practice of communion with the Lord[94] in the morning. David, the psalmist, states: "In the morning, Lord, you hear my voice; in the morning I lay my requests before you and wait expectantly." Both Jesus and David serve as model reminders that before we get distracted and face the myriad of things that want to invade our peace that is promised, we must go to the Source as the first order of our day.

This weekly Sabbath and early daily time with your Maker will become your favorite time of your day. This sacred time will be savored and special to you. As you begin to make this your habit, you will be saying in agreement with the man who had a heart after God's own heart, "You lead me in the path of life. I experience absolute joy in your presence; you always give me sheer delight."[95] Taste and see, my friends![96]

FASTING:
GOOD FOR BODY AND
SOUL

◆ ◆ ◆

The writer has been in the church his entire life, attending three academic Christian institutions (undergraduate and graduate levels), and has never heard this topic preached or addressed save on two occasions. The first was at Simpson Memorial Church, now called Living Christ Church, in Nyack, NY. Pastor Neal Clarke gave a sermon on "fasting." The Biblical text he preached was from Matthew 6; it was eye-opening. Pastor Clarke addressed medical concerns that one might have and gave a cautionary word. Nonetheless, he was faithful to the words of Jesus and challenged us to practice what Jesus said. The writer took the challenge.

The second time the writer heard the same challenge was many years later on *The 700*

Club (CBN). Pat Robertson was interviewing his guest, a nationally recognized cardiologist, Chauncey Crandall, M.D. Dr. Crandall cited the cardiovascular benefits of fasting, and the spiritual advantages as well. In the interview, Dr. Crandall cited two observations. One from WWII, where POWs (prisoners of war) were placed on a "forced fast" because they were deprived, and they had a limited food intake. Many of these individuals he cited, who went into the concentration camps with heart disease, came out without heart disease. Dr. Crandall continued stating that individuals in the Mormon Church who practiced regular fasting had a 30 percent reduction in heart disease as well.

The benefits of fasting to the body are many, as we will discuss later. At the same time, the writer wants to excite and ignite your interest to the spiritual power that is available to you through the practice of fasting. The writer will share a true story about the power that is unleashed and wielded through fasting. He will also highlight an even greater miraculous story by Dr. Crandall that he later wrote about.

Ben Waller has been attending our men's group for several years. Ben has been presenting to our group a series on a "Healthier Temple," as the author has cited before. The work is well-researched and is providential to this writing. It is in outline form and is best presented and understood in the same manner.

I. WHAT IS REGULAR FASTING?

    a. The abstinence from food and drink, except water, for a set amount of time.

    b. It typically takes twelve hours after your last meal to fully enter the fasted state. Once in the fasted state, good things happen:

        1. Your body will start to burn stored body fat, which is normally inaccessible unless you're in a fasted state.

        2. Detoxification of the body toxins typically stored in body fat are dissolved and removed from the body.

        3. The body reboots the entire immune

system, purging the old, damaged, or inefficient parts of the immune system, and at the same time boosting the production of new healthy white blood cells.

- Studies have shown that even a prior seventy-two-hour fast was enough to help protect cancer patients from the harmful and toxic effects of chemotherapy treatments.

4. Cognitive brain function, memory, learning, clarity, and alertness are all increased with fasting.

- It makes sense why Jesus promoted fasting for Himself and His followers during His ministry.

- Pythagoras, the Greek mathematician, would require his students to fast before his lectures, because he felt they would not understand his teaching without the benefits of fasting!

II. HISTORY OF FASTING

a. Fasting is one of the most ancient healing traditions in human history. This solution has been practiced by virtually every culture and religion on earth.

b. Fasting dates to 460-370 BC with the Greek philosopher and physician Hippocrates, who has been called "the father of medicine" and who taught the importance of fasting and would prescribe it often. He stated, "To eat when you're sick is to feed your illness."

c. Fasting is mentioned over fifty times in the Bible, in both the Old (Hebrew Scriptures) and New Testaments.

1. Matthew 6:16, where Jesus is teaching His disciples basic principles of godly living. Jesus begins with "When you fast," not "If you fast," implying that fasting will be a regular practice within His followers' lives.

d. Today, fasting is becoming more mainstream, not just for religious reasons but also as a modality in the preventative medicine and healthy living sector of society.

III. WHY FAST?

   a. Health Benefits of Fasting

     1. Boosts immune system

     2. Detoxifies the body

     3. Lowers blood pressure

     4. Lowers cholesterol

     5. Stimulates brain function, focus, and clarity

     6. Positive impact on mental wellbeing (due to increased endorphins released)

     7. Increases insulin sensitivity (reduces risk for diabetes)

     8. Weight loss

     9. Improves longevity and health span

     10. Rejuvenates skin

     11. Increases HGH (human growth hor-

mone) which makes us young and vibrant[97]

12. Reduces heart disease[98]

13. Fasting turns on "good" genes and turns "off" our bad genes, a process called epigenetics[99]

14. Accelerates autophagy (the clean-up of aged and damaged cells)[100]

b. Biblical Reasons for Fasting

1. Fasting prepares you for the works God has ordained for you to do.

2. There are many circumstances one would fast for, as cited in the Bible:

- Worship God – Luke 2:37
- Prepare for ministry – Matthew 4:1-17, Luke 4:1-14
- Seek God's wisdom – Acts 14:23
- Show grief – Nehemiah -1:1-4
- Seek deliverance or protection – Ezra 8:21-23
- Repent – Jonah 3:5-10

- Gain victory – Judges 20:26

IV. TYPES OF FASTING

  a. Intermittent fasting (most popular)

    1. 16/8 fasting method (fast for 16 hours daily) – fasting for 16 hours and feeding for 8 hours per 24-hour day

- Example: fast from 8 p.m. to 12 p.m. the next day (16 hours), then eat only between 12 noon and 8 p.m. daily. (Women do better with 14/10.)

- One can drink water, (black) coffee, or tea without anything added, and no solid food during the fast.

- Within the eating window, fit in 2-3 meals.

- It is important to eat healthy foods during the eating windows, not junk food or excessive amounts of calories.

    2. Eat-Stop-Eat (24-hour fast, once or

twice a week)

- Continuous 24-hour fast, either once or twice a week.
- Example: fasting from dinner to dinner, breakfast to breakfast, lunch to lunch.
- Can drink water, (black) coffee, or tea without anything added, and no solid food.
- Very important to eat healthy and normally during eating periods; meaning eating the same amount of food as if you hadn't been fasting at all.

3. 5/2 fasting diet—eating recommended calorie intake for 5 days a week but reducing daily calorie intake to 25% for the remaining 2 days (600 calories for men and 500 calories for women per day)

b. Prolonged fasting

c. 24+ hours (multiple days) of a continuous fast

- It is important to work up slowly to 24+ hour fasting.
- Drink plenty of water to avoid dehydration.
- Coffee without sugar or cream (black) or tea without anything added is okay.
- Performed less frequently, i.e. monthly or bimonthly.

c. Time-Restricted feeding (i.e. break-fast: the meal that breaks your fast)

1. Set a specific time period for eating; for example, between 9 a.m. and 5 p.m., or only 12 p.m. to 5 p.m., etc.

d. Fasting Mimicking Diet (Prolon) www. Prolonfmd.com

1. 5-day nutritional program which nourishes your body while promoting the regenerative and rejuvenating changes of a 5-day fast.

V. Precautions when fasting:

a. Children should NEVER fast

b. Pregnant and nursing women should NEVER fast

c. Those who should consult a doctor or be under his/her care during fasting include the following:

1. The extremely frail

2. Those with a weakened immune system

3. Persons with eating disorders

4. Persons with medication-dependent diabetes, heart disease, or high blood pressure

   • Fasting will naturally lower your blood pressure, so you would not want to take your normal, full dosage of blood pressure medicine as it might drop your blood pressure too low, and needs to be monitored by your doctor.

- Insulin sensitivity improves with fasting, so you will typically use less diabetic medication while fasting, so this will need to be monitored closely and adjusted by your doctor.
- Individuals on diuretics or blood thinners

5. Persons on lengthy, prolonged water fasting should always be monitored by a doctor.

VI. TIPS TO GET STARTED

a. Choose what type of fast works best for you.

b. Ease into it—start with shorter fasts and work up to longer periods

c. Plan and be flexible

d. Prepare for your body to feel different during the fast

1. Cardio exercise in a fasted state will accelerate fat-burning benefits and is okay; however, strength training

should only be done during your feeding state, i.e. when you are doing intermittent fasting.

Fasting allows one to get closer to the Lord and hear from Him more readily. Why, you ask? It feeds the spirit and mortifies the flesh. Which one wins is the one you feed. Like two dogs that fight—the one that gets fed is going to win, because he is stronger. When we feed our spirit through worship, the Word, fellowship, and fasting, we feed our spirit and weaken our flesh so that we our led by the Spirit and not our flesh.

Moreover, one of the byproducts is spiritual power. The writer had been practicing fasting as discussed. A couple of years ago, in a place of business, he was asked to pray for a woman who was having some medical issues and needed some healing. Only Jesus and Jesus alone heals. With that said, Jesus is pleased to use people who believe that He is the same today; He still wants to heal.

The writer asked the woman if she was

saved, which is the most important of all decisions that we make. Moreover, he investigated to see if there was any unforgiveness that she had toward anyone, especially toward her ex-husband. Jesus made it abundantly clear that unforgiveness toward others obstructs our prayers and brings the Father's discipline on His children.[101]

All of this she had done, so the writer proceeded to anoint her with the anointing oil that he carries with him for such occasions. As he finished anointing her and began a simple prayer that Jesus would heal her according to His Word, she began to "manifest," meaning she had a demon and began screaming that it was choking her. The author had not encountered anything like this before, individually. He got scared for about five to ten seconds. His eyes were wide as saucers for sure, with the shock of the reaction of the woman in torment.

Then, coming to his senses, he got angry—very angry. Angry at this devil for tormenting this woman in this way. He remembered and realized that he had authority in Christ, was fully anointed in God the Holy Spirit, and he was a MOG (man of God), and that sucker was going to go! Demons have no choice but to submit to the name and authority of King Jesus. So many Christians know the Great Commission in Matthew 28:19. Yet they miss the most important basis for our sending, stated in verse 18 (NIV), where Jesus states, "All authority in heaven and on earth has been given to Me. Therefore go." We are to go and do His work in His authority on earth, bringing His kingdom's rule and reign here on the real estate where we walk.

There is a close link between fasting and hearing Jesus' voice and functioning in the power of the Holy Spirit. Fasting is a God-given gateway to enter this kind of kingdom activity in your life. Unfortunately, most Christians in the United States do not get it, and therefore miss out on kingdom living. The writer believes that is not the case for you, the reader of this book—otherwise you would not be reading this book, for the sovereign Father wants you to hear this. As you hunger for more of the supernatural power of the Holy Spirit, He will show up in your life in ways that will leave you in awe and wonder.

The writer's story is pale compared to Dr. Chauncey Crandall's. For his book *Raising the Dead: A Doctor Encounters the Miraculous*, Dr. Crandall was featured on *The 700 Club* a few years ago, sharing the benefits of fasting from his clinical experience as a cardiologist. As a Christian, he also cited the benefits to one's faith as well. Then he related the story, as the title of the book states, of a miraculous encounter that all (the Holy Spirit shows no favoritism) disciples of Christ can do in His power.

A relatively young male walked into the hospital one day clutching his chest, as Dr. Crandall related the story. The man later coded, and they worked several times to revive him without success. Dr. Crandall had associates and nurses there at the scene, and he called the time of death. As Dr. Crandall began to leave the ER and go through the double doors, he heard an inaudible voice tell him to go back and put the paddles on the man one more time. He admits he was startled by the word he received, yet he acted on it. To the surprise of his co-workers, he asked them to join him in this—yet another attempt to revive this dead man. Well, you can surmise the surprise—when they placed the paddles on the dead man and his heart began to beat, the nurse screamed with shock!

Why does the writer mention this event, you ask? Well, Dr. Crandall mentioned on the same program (*The 700 Club*) the benefits of fasting; one of which is a closeness to Christ and the ensuing power and authority because of that closeness to Christ.

HE IS GOD:
THE HOLY SPIRIT

◆ ◆ ◆

Tradition can sometimes be a hindrance to our walk with the living Lord when we place it over Scripture. When Scripture is not the final authority for our faith and lifestyle, it can create some problems for us. That was the case for the writer's great-grandfather, who was a denominational minister who placed greater value on the denomination and its traditions than on the supremacy of the organic Word of God.

This led Reverend Joseph Harvey, during the WWII period, to leave his denomination and establish a church near a military base in the state of Florida. Reverend Harvey's wish was to form a church "for the unity of all Christians." The church's by-laws also reflected his wish. They state, "This Church shall have no denominational test of fellowship and is committed to the discipleship of Jesus Christ as Lord and Savior, and to His great commandments as the Christian way of life."

You may say, this is interesting, but how is this related to the Holy Spirit? There is a close relationship between unity and the Person of the Holy Spirit! God the Holy Spirit is not an "it," but a Person, with a will, personality, and infinite intellect. At the same time, He is very God of God. We do not see Him because He is a Spirit, which causes some Christians to doubt His presence and activity in their lives, to their own loss.

The Bible addresses two areas that impact the presence and power of the Spirit in our lives. We can grieve the Holy Spirit in our relationships through the six sins that Saint Paul cites: bitterness, anger, wrath, quarreling, evil, and slanderous talk. The apostle then states three positives that we should practice: "Be kind to one another, compassionate, forgiving one another, just as God in Christ also forgave you"[102]

The second area that impacts the presence and power of the Holy Spirit in us is quenching Him. Again, the Bible states through Paul: "Do not quench the Spirit"[103]; another translation states: "Do not extinguish the Spirit." God the Holy Spirit is the living, sovereign Being who does not force Himself on us. He only works where He is welcomed and wanted. You may say that He is the finest of gentlemen; He does not force Himself on us. He shows up where He is celebrated and worshipped; not just acknowledged as some dogma or idea to concede to.

When we, as followers of Christ, fan the flame of the Spirit, it activates His presence and power in a supernatural way. The apostle Paul makes this clear with the very next verse after the one that was previously stated: "Do not treat prophecies with contempt. But test everything."[104]

The reality of the power of the Spirit and His manifestation became a reality to the writer, not just a concept. He was invited to participate in a nationally televised crusade in 2011 held in Dallas, Texas. Three well-recognized, spirit-filled men from Argentina—Carlos Annacondia, Sergio Scataglini, and Professor Claudio Freidzon—along with prophet/teacher Cindy Jacobs and pastor Sam Hinn, were the featured speakers, engaging in active ministry, praying for healing and casting out demons; things the writer only had read about in seminary but was an eyewitness to at this crusade.

The writer was prayed for, along with many other local Christian leaders, for a greater anointing of the Holy Spirit. Immediately after the writer went through the line as these men prayed for us, the author felt overwhelmed by a Presence; he had to lean against a wall to steady himself.

Shortly afterward, he joined his friends who were in attendance from his men's group. They knew that he had been prayed for. One of the men in this small group of friends had recently gone through a difficult divorce. The writer felt led to pray for him with the other men in the group. He placed his hand on the man's heart, symbolically asking Jesus to heal his broken heart. While praying for the man, the man fell forward, leaning on the writer's hand… the author and the Holy Spirit were holding the man up when he was overcome by the power of God the Holy Spirit. Needless to say, the author was amazed at what took place, and the other men witnessed what took place as well.

Within a few minutes after this took place, the author felt compelled to say something. The "urge" and conviction became stronger every moment, until the writer could no longer contain the message. "Ken is going to raise the dead." Again, he said it louder, and with more conviction and authority: "Ken is going to raise the dead." The writer sounded like a loud parrot, stating the same thing over and over again. When he stopped, he asked Ken, "What do you think of that word?" Ken replied, "The Lord already revealed that to me in a dream!" Ken was a MOG (man of God) and had already been in ministry many years and had seen many miracles and healings.

The writer was a police chaplain for many years and came to know an officer through the tragic death of his young son. This officer recommended the writer to minister to another law enforcement officer from another state. The officer's teenage son had fallen off a bridge in Dallas while drunk, falling many feet onto the concrete street below and hitting his head. Consequently, I was called to come and pray for Ryan. I could not make the call because I was on another emergency call to another local hospital, so I called Ken.

Ryan's mother was a woman of great faith. She specially asked for a "Pentecostal preacher" to come and pray for Ryan. The writer knew that Ken could meet that request, so he made the call to Ken, who has a heart for officers—as he himself is a retired captain of a large sheriff's department, a former chaplain, and an ordained minister. The MOG (man of God) that Ken is said yes, and said he would keep me appraised of the situation. When he arrived, he found Ryan in the ICU, on life support and brain-dead.

Ken prayed for Ryan many times over several weeks. Jesus commands us to ask and keep on asking in faith, with the expectation that He will do what He has already said He will do. Within a few weeks, Ryan's mom called the writer to thank him and sent him a video of Ryan, talking and fully recovered! Jesus is awesome, and He is looking for men, women, boys, and girls of mustard seed faith who will take Him at His Word. Ken was that willing servant! The anointing that Ken has is available to all; God the Holy Spirit shows no favoritism—He is just seeking individuals from every walk of life and any age that hunger for His filling and power!

This took place about a year after the writer had prophesied that Ken would raise the dead! Interestingly, several years ago Ken was visiting Texas, and he stopped by our men's group and gave an update about what the Lord is doing in his ministry. He shared that he has raised (through the power of the Holy Spirit) two more individuals who were clinically dead and were being sustained by life support!

The sovereign King Jesus has commissioned and commanded us to do what He did and to occupy and expand His real estate until He returns. Our King has given us power to do all these supernatural works today. In His last words to us before He left the earth, He said, "But you will receive power when the Holy Spirit comes on you."[105]

Most Christians believe, erroneously, that these supernatural activities are reserved for some "super-Christians." The Lord is scanning His earth, looking for individuals who will take Him at His Word. Just a mustard seed amount of faith in His unfailing Word is all that is necessary to do everything in the Bible today.[106] Jesus has not changed; what He has done in the past, He still wants to do today! Faith is what moves the Lord's miraculous hand. The Bible says that without it we cannot please Him.[107]

One of my favorite stories is from my professor, Howard Hendricks, at Dallas Theological Seminary. Dr. Hendricks personally mentored many of the evangelical leaders we hear and see today on the radio and TV. Dr. Hendricks had a national ministry and a very busy schedule in addition to his work at Dallas

Seminary. Dr. Hendricks relayed to us that in addition to all of this public ministry, He was discipling a homeless man—one on one.

Prof. Hendricks gave the homeless man a New Testament (it included the Psalms and Proverbs) and asked the man to read the gospel of John. The man returned to Prof. Hendricks in a couple of weeks. Consequently, Prof. Hendricks asked him, "Did you read it?" The homeless man responded, "Yes, I read the whole thing, including the 'palms' (the Psalms) and the 'pro-burbs' (the Proverbs)!" Then the man said this: "Can I do everything written in this Book?" Dr. Hendricks said to us, musing aloud, "I could have gone down the dispensational fire-escape, but I said to him, 'That is what it says (you can do).'" Indeed, that is what it says, and we all can do what it says we can do through God the Holy Spirit!

HEAVEN: NOT THE SAME FOR EVERYBODY

◆ ◆ ◆

Most people have false assumptions of heaven. Their understanding of heaven has been shaped by the culture of movies, music, cartoons, and the jesters of our day. People often joke of things that they do not understand or feel threatened by.

However, once you understand what the Bible says regarding heaven, it will transform your life. It will give you a new purpose and a sense of urgency, and will cause you to make the most of your time here on earth; for what we do now has eternal consequences.

Heaven Is Not a Democracy

Most Christians in America have the view that if they make it to heaven, that is great. They are not excited about the prospect of heaven. They see it as a place of perpetual boredom, floating around on a cloud, singing songs to Jesus in this ethereal and surreal existence filled with endless singing. Jesus' message was very clear and incapable of falsehood or error. Jesus stated simply that heaven is a place. This "place" is the Greek word topos, from which we get our English word *topography*. This place is being prepared now by our Master as He stated, "And if I go and prepare a place for you, I will come back and take you to be with Me that you also may be where I am."[108] This place is being uniquely prepared for each individual believer based on what we are doing now for our King.

Our enjoyment of the place called heaven will be based on what we do with our time, treasures, and talents that the Father has given each believer in Christ. Please note that the writer did not say that our entrance into heaven is based on works. The Bible is very clear that salvation is by grace alone. The apostle Paul states: "For it is by grace you have been saved, through faith—and this is not from yourselves, it is the gift of God—not by works, so that no one can boast."[109] Thus, the Bible is very clear that we cannot work nor earn our salvation. Our entrance into heaven is solely a work of God through the cross of Christ.

Art can be a powerful medium in conveying truth. At the university the writer attended, he lived in the dorms. One semester he lived in a dorm that had a huge mural painted on the building's hallway. Every time you were waiting for the elevators you would find yourself looking at this large, skillfully-drawn picture. The picture was of the Peanuts character Charlie Brown. It depicted Charlie Brown alone in a large classroom, fast asleep at his desk. The caption above him had the following words: "Sometimes it's too early to learn, but it's never too late!" This has been the case for the author about the importance of our future destiny. Please do not let this be the case for you. Our time here is critically precious! Jesus' own half-brother James did not get the message, because he too was asleep with unbelief—until later. If you remember, he was one of the family members who tried to restrain Jesus because he thought Jesus was out of his mind. Later, however, this same James woke up from his unbelief and became one of the pillars of the Church, imploring all Christians throughout the centuries to make the most of our brief time on earth.[110]

With the foundation of salvation by grace and grace alone established, the apostle Paul writes to believers about another foundational truth that will transform their earthly existence and make their time in eternity more than what one could imagine! Writing to Christians, Paul states: "Therefore, my dear friends, as you have always obeyed—not only in my presence, but now much more in my absence—continue to work out your salvation with fear and trembling, for it is God who works in you to will and to act in order to fulfill His good purpose."[111]

Every individual who has received the gracious gift of new birth in Jesus Christ has been given a charge, a challenge, and a privilege to serve our Master out of gratitude for being a recipient of fullness of life, now and forevermore! Furthermore, as we "work out our salvation" in service to our Lord, He rewards us at the "awards ceremony" in heaven called the Judgment Seat (Bema) of Christ. This event, that every believer will enjoy, will be the deciding factor for the rewards we receive, and the privileges, position, and praise we enjoy for all of eternity!

Saint Paul, writing to the believers at Corinth, explains this future event that all Christians will participate in. Paul states: "For we must all appear before the judgment seat of Christ, so that each of us may receive what is due us for the things done while in the body, whether good or bad."[112] Our works are going to be evaluated—whether they are good, or worthless. The Greek word phaulon is better translated as "worthless" than "bad." Paul continues explaining this time of evaluation by the Lord Himself of our works of service for Him. Paul states: "If anyone builds on this foundation using gold, silver, costly stones, wood, hay or straw, their work will be shown for what it is, because the Day (of evaluation) will bring it to light. It will be revealed with fire, and the fire will test the quality of each person's work. If what has been built survives, the builder will receive a reward. If it is burned up, the builder will suffer loss but yet will be saved—even though only as one escaping through the flames."[113] Thus, the Bible is clear that there are rewards for our work in the body. At the same time, some believers will suffer loss for their work due to disobedience, sinful motives, or sinful methods. Jesus will test the quality of our work!

The loss of reward will be felt for eternity! The Lord is anxious to reward His servants for their service to Him. However, much of the Church is like Charlie Brown—asleep, with no idea of what they are doing and not doing. Not realizing that this short time on earth is a training ground for the new creation that Jesus is preparing now for each of us, based upon what we do with the divine help He has given us today.

On *The 700 Club* Pat Robertson interviewed Dr. Hugh Ross, an astrophysicist, about his latest book, *The Creator and the Cosmos*, subtitled *How the Greatest Scientific Discoveries of the Century Reveal God*. Interestingly, Dr. Ross stated some points that he wanted followers of Christ to grasp. Specifically, that God has a purpose for each believer in Christ; this is not going to be the believer's final career here on earth. Dr. Ross continued by saying that God has a new career for every Christian in the new creation—more than they can imagine. As Christians, we will be ruling over God's creation. Dr. Ross pointed out that even the angels watch the grace of God we experience.[114]

Jesus: "Look, I am coming soon! My reward is with Me" (Revelation 22:12 NIV).

This is what Jesus has told us as believers; it is imperative that we heed His call to action. We the Church, corporately and individually, are loved and treasured by Him. Jesus wants us to enjoy the new heaven and new earth that He is creating for each member that makes up His beautiful Bride, the Church. Jesus has told us the prize that awaits believers for what they have accomplished with the time, treasures, and talents He has entrusted to His followers.

Jesus gives every believer today a challenge: "Look, I am coming soon! My reward is with Me, and I will give to each person according to what they have done."[115] This begs the question, "What are you and I doing now for the King whom we say we love and obey?"

The apostle Paul states that we who are born again are in a race to receive awards. Paul states: "Do you not know that in a race all the runners run, but only one gets the prize? Run in such a way as to get the prize. Everyone who competes in the games goes into strict training. They do it to get a crown that will not last, but we do it to get a crown that will last forever."[116] In Paul's day, the athletes that competed in the games did so to earn crowns that were actually wreaths of pine and celery that would perish within a few days. Paul is using that fact to contrast the "crowns" that we can earn that are imperishable and eternal!

As disciples of Christ, Jesus is going to reward us with "crowns" for our acts of service to Him. The New Testament scholar Gerhard Kittel explains that these crowns are signs and symbols that are formed of imperishable leaves that form a halo that represents awarded joy and glory.[117]

The New Testament mentions five crowns that will be awarded by Jesus at His Judgment Seat. The Greek word translated "crown" is stephanon. This term was employed in the Greek games in New Testament times, as stated. It referred to a wreath that was awarded to the sole victor in the games that took place. The New Testament writers took this term to picture for believers then and now the temporary crowns awarded in athletic contests, in contrast to eternal crowns that can be awarded to us if we do what is required—as stated in Scripture—to receive them.

The first crown is the "crown of life." James, the half-brother of Jesus, describes how we may acquire this crown: "Blessed (happy) is the one who perseveres under trial because, having stood the test, that person will receive the crown of life that the Lord has promised to those who love Him."[118] This same crown, the crown of life, is also mentioned in Revelation

2:20, again with the same theme—persevering in the midst of difficulties.

As something to note, when the Bible repeats something, it is important. When God chooses to repeat a Word, He wants to make sure that we get it! Sometimes our ears become plugged up with "the wax of unbelief" which prevents the Word from being received, processed, and obeyed.

This crown is available to all believers who face difficulties for obeying Christ in difficult circumstances. The crown comes with a condition, however: persevering during difficulty. All followers of Christ will face "trials," and thus all are given this opportunity to receive this "crown of life" if we endure our trials with love for Him! Please note that this crown, with its privileges, praise, and position (we will expand on this later) is available to all; Jesus shows no favoritism!

The Lord gives the means to endure and rewards us with a crown too! The means the Lord grants us is His grace: "God's Resources At Christ's Expense" (G.R.A.C.E.). In short, supernatural help!

The second crown that we can receive at the Judgment Seat of Christ is the "crown of glory." This crown is available to those who serve as faithful examples of leadership within the Church. This would include but is not limited to pastors, teachers, elders, deacons, youth leaders, and those who have leadership roles in the many parachurch ministries. This is a radiant crown that never fades away, as the apostle Peter states.[119]

The third crown is the "crown of exultation." This crown is the fruit of discipleship. It is all the people you have invested in discipling who are bearing fruit for the kingdom. Therefore, the apostle Paul states of these individuals that he had poured himself into: "For you are our glory and joy!"[120] As a boat cuts through the water in a lake and leaves waves behind, forming a wake, we too leave a wake, as the maxim states. But the Bible would add another perspective by saying that we all leave an eternal wake through the lives we bring to heaven and those we encourage along the way. Jesus is pleased to award us with a crown for this!

The fourth crown is the "imperishable crown." Paul uses something most of us can relate to—competition. He draws a picture of runners in a stadium, running in a race, striving to win the prize. Paul continues to develop the idea further by saying that each runner exercises self-control in everything, focusing on the prize that awaits the winner. Then he says something that is radical and revolutionary: "Run in such a way that you may win"[121]! The next verse reveals the award: a crown that is not temporal but is eternal and "imperishable." That, my friends, is worth running for! But we must leave our seats in the stadium and get in the race!

We all need reminders to keep us focused on the prize and keep us from distractions. The writer is a member of the CMA (Christian Motorcycle Association). They publish a monthly magazine with a Christian perspective and a missionary emphasis. They customarily have a full-page picture that contains a Scripture verse. The writer found and framed one picture and placed it in a prominent place in the garage as a reminder of the apostle Paul's challenge to win. The picture displays a rider on a sport-bike on a racetrack, getting ready to race. It captures the rider smoking the rear tire; getting the motorcycle ready to race. CMA placed this Bible verse within the picture: "Don't you realize that in a race everyone runs, but only one person gets the prize? So run to win!"[122]

The fifth crown is the "crown of righteousness" that awaits a certain group of Christians. The apostle Paul placed himself in this group with the expectation of receiving this crown of righteousness. In 2 Timothy 4, Paul reminds Timothy, whom he has been grooming in the faith, "I have competed well; I have finished the race; I have kept the faith!"[123] Because of that fact, Paul declares that he has something reserved for him. Yes, the "crown of righteousness."

Consequently, what is exciting to note is Paul's closing word. After finishing his thought about his coming "crown of righteousness," he gives an exciting word for us. The apostle states: "[He] will award it to me in that day (the Judgment Seat)—and not to me only, but also to all who have set their affection on His appearing."[124] Paul tells us that those who have loved and longed for Jesus' appearing will be awarded this "crown of righteousness." And why should we, as His Bride, not long for and love the coming of our King, who has prepared a place beyond description for us to be with Him?

In his book *Perfect Ending: Why Your Eternal Future Matters Today*, Dr. Robert Jeffress clearly outlines for us the privileges, praise, and positions some believers will enjoy for eternity. These rewards of privilege, praise, and position are contingent upon our works passing the test at the Judgment Seat of Christ, where the quality of each person's work will be tested. The apostle Paul reveals what this evaluation of our rewards (not heaven itself) will entail. Paul states: "Their (the believer's) work will be shown for what it is, because the Day will bring it to light. It will be revealed with fire, and the fire will test the quality of each person's work... If (conditional) it is burned up, the builder (the believer) will suffer loss but yet will be saved—even though only as one escaping through the flames."[125]

Privilege: Dr. Jeffress states that some believers will be granted a special entrance into the kingdom of God (2 Peter 1:11), special access to the tree of life (Revelation 2:7), and even special treatment by Christ Himself (Luke 12:37). He finishes with the statement that "these benefits are real and worth attaining."[126]

Praise: all of us appreciate recognition for work well done. Can you recall when you were in middle school or high school, when your teacher praised you for your good work? Or when your mom or dad praised you for something you did that pleased them greatly? We are made in the Father's likeness. The Father praised His Son on the commencement of His ministry. "This is my Son, whom I love; with Him I am well pleased."[127]

If Jesus was pleased to hear such praise from the Father, we will enjoy such praise from Him as well. Dr. Jeffress states: "Imagine the Creator of the universe looking at you and stating those wonderful words: 'Well done, good and faithful servant!'"[128] Dr. Jeffress notes, "This reward will be reserved for obedient Christians."[129]

Position: another tangible reward that some will enjoy for eternity; something that we cannot fathom with our finite minds, yet it is just as real as our world is now. These rewards of position will be for ever and ever! Jesus always spoke truth and is incapable of falsehood or mistakes. Jesus states: "You have been faithful with a few things; I will put you in charge of many things."[130]

Dr. Jeffress explains further by saying, "Jesus is teaching that our faithfulness in this life will determine what responsibility we have in the new heaven and earth. Paul declared this truth as well in 2 Timothy 2:12: 'If we endure, we will also reign with Him.' One day we will be co-rulers with Christ over the angels, the planets, and the nations."[131]

Most Christians fail to understand what

we will be doing in the new heaven and earth. God has given us a small portrait in Genesis 2 with Adam and Eve, where they had unbroken fellowship and intimacy with the Father. He placed them in a garden that was temperate and lush with beauty, teeming with life, and with all the food they could ever want at their fingertips. No sin was present, and everything functioned perfectly.

During all this, their Father gave them an assignment—work. God said of this "work" that it was very good. Why? There were no obstacles to their work. The obstacles came later, after their disobedience to the Father. God Himself worked for six days in creation. Work brings meaning and purpose to our lives. Why do we think life in the new heaven and earth will be any different? Work will be more fulfilling, without fractured relationships and bodies that get tired and sick.

Like Adam and Eve, we were made in the likeness of God. God is a creator, sustainer, and builder. The Father charged the first couple to "tend the Garden." Literally, they were charged to have dominion and rule over the real estate where He placed them. They ruled and had assignments that were bestowed on them as a blessing to enjoy. Likewise, this is how it will be for us if we faithfully serve our Father now, wherever He has placed us, to do whatever good works which He has prepared us to do here on this temporal place called earth. If we are faithful in this life, we will enjoy unimaginable rewards that we cannot fully comprehend. Both Jesus and the apostle Paul urged us powerfully to heed their invitation to partake of these rewards and not to suffer loss!

THE BEST NEWS

◆ ◆ ◆

God has placed three questions and imprinted them in the human heart. When the Hebrew Scripture (the Old Testament) uses the word heart, it refers more than to the wonderful cardiac muscle that beats in your chest; rather, heart refers to one's "intellect, emotions, and will."[132] With this in mind, your Creator and mine has placed within each beating heart three questions that long to be answered.

The first question is: "Where did I come from?" The second follows the first: "Why am I here?" Which invariably leads to the third question: "Where am I going?" The answers cannot be found on Google. They are found in God's Holy Word, the Bible. It is a source like no other, and it never changes. "Your word, LORD, is eternal; it stands firm in the heavens."[133]

The first question is addressed by a man who was known all over the world for his wisdom; people sought him from foreign lands for his wisdom, given by the Lord Himself. Solomon states that "He (God) has also set eternity in the human heart."[134] Your dog who looks up to you—or your cat that looks down at you—has no innate sense of eternity like us humans do. They are special to us, no doubt, judging by all the time, affection, and money we spend on them. Nonetheless, they are not pondering the three questions previously stated, because God has not placed eternity in their hearts!

Our Maker has placed those eternal questions in our hearts to lead us to Him. The sovereign One, who threw the stars into place on the black velvet canvas of the universe, wants to have a relationship with you and me. Imagine that the One who formed all that we see—and the seven or eight billion people that He has made, each one uniquely made with different fingerprints—knows you by name and longs to have a relationship with you! How awesome is the fact that the Maker and Sustainer of all things longs to have an intimate relationship with us!

God has answered those eternal questions in His Word, and in the Person of Jesus Christ. Jesus Christ, the Son of God, answers these eternal questions that plague the human heart which seeks the answers to these questions.

The first one: "Where did I come from?" is answered in Psalm 139, when King David was inspired by God the Holy Spirit to pen his origins and ours. Scripture states: "For You created my inmost being; You knit me together in my mother's womb. I praise You because I am fearfully and wonderfully made."[135] David is making it clear that the Lord made us, and that we are a product of His divine handiwork through our mother and father, and that each of us are thus "wonderfully made."

The second question, "Why am I here?" addresses the "soul hunger" that every person feels and that nothing satisfies, save for the One who made us. No relationship, success, achievement, toys, or any material thing will satisfy the vacuum our Maker has left in our hearts that He and only He alone can fill. God longs to have a relationship with us, to commune with us, and to have the intimacy that every soul longs for—intimacy without fear, and a love that is like no other. It is a joy unspeakable and full of glory that is beyond description. It is real—very real—and is available for all who wish to experience it!

Jesus alone promised to fill that soul hunger. He gave an open invitation to every person who will receive His offer. Jesus was talking to the crowd of people who were looking for another physical meal of bread from Him. But Jesus knew that they needed more than physical bread; they needed the Bread of Life. "Then Jesus declared, 'I am the bread of life. Whoever comes to me will never go hungry, and whoever believes in Me will never be thirsty.'"[136] Another man who was a playboy and a "party animal" of his day had a radical encounter with Christ and was totally transformed by Him; he understood the question "Why am I here?" Saint Augustine said, "You have made us for

Yourself, and our hearts are restless until they rest in You."

Most professing Christians miss the invitation and the claim that Jesus is making. So many people think that Jesus is offering them "fire insurance," and they believe that they have that "box" checked. Jesus came as Savior and Lord. He does not give any disciple of His the option of just accepting Him as Savior alone. His invitation is to be the very staple of our lives—every part of our lives. Lord of all. Only then do we enjoy the intimacy, enjoyment, and the dining privileges that He offers with Him at the dining table of His presence.[137]

The third question is the final and eternal question: "Where am I going?" The Bible is very clear in its message—everyone born here on planet earth is going to live forever. It is not a debatable issue in God's Word. The same Bible makes clear that we get to choose the location where we dwell for eternity! God longs for us to be with Him, a holy God. But His justice demands payment for our individual sin. God knew that we could not pay the penalty for our sin that His holiness and perfection requires. Therefore, because of His overwhelming love, He allowed His sinless and holy Son to take your place and mine, to pay the debt that had to be paid for our sin. This was paid on a cruel cross around 33 AD at a stone hill in Jerusalem called Golgotha, meaning "place of the skull." This "skull" hill is still visible today— next to an Arab bus station now.

Two thousand years later, you can still see the dark and eerie image of a skull in this hill pictured here in Israel. As archaeologists state: "The stones cry out to the truth." Golgotha stands as a historical marker and a reminder of where and what Jesus did for all who choose to receive this gracious gift of forgiveness.

The positive consequence of our decision is life to the full now, and eternity in heaven. Our minds cannot comprehend fully a life with no more time, sickness, sorrow, or pain—and with joy inexpressible! The Bible gives us a glimpse of what is to come for all who choose to receive Christ as Savior and Lord. "Then I saw 'a new heaven and a new earth,' for the first heaven and the first earth had passed away... God's dwelling place is now among the people, and He will dwell with them. They will be His people, and God Himself will be with them and be their God. He will wipe every tear from their eyes. There will be no more death or mourning or crying or pain, for the old order of things has passed away."[138] Jesus has prepared and reserved in His Father's house a place for all who invite Him to be their Savior and Lord. How awesome is the offer which He offers to all!

Furthermore, Jesus states clearly that "I am going there (back to heaven) to prepare a place for you."[139] Jesus is now in a "place" (a real location) called heaven, engaged in a massive building project that is customized for you. Jesus knows you best and loves you the most of anyone you know—including yourself! He knows what will bring you the most joy and is handcrafting a place designed and built uniquely for you.

C.S. Lewis describes heaven this way when he states: "Your place in heaven will seem to be made for you and you alone, because you were made for it—made for it stitch by stitch, as a glove is made for a hand."[140] If that does not motivate you to live every moment of your life to please Him, please check your pulse!

Nonetheless, there is more to the message of Jesus that much of the Church in America is uncomfortable with. As communicators of the Words of Jesus, we must proclaim the complete message He gave, not just the parts we like. We do not get to practice "cafeteria Christianity," picking and choosing the Words of Christ we like to follow like food on a buffet line.

Please know that no one loves people more than Jesus does. Jesus even loves you more than you love yourself! This is a profoundly important truth about Him that is critical to embrace. Furthermore, no one has communicated better than Jesus did or was brighter and more winsome than He. Unfortunately, many pastors throughout the US think they know better and are afraid of offending people in churches, and thus avoid mentioning what Jesus described more than any other person in the Bible. Consequently, we are editing the words of Jesus— thinking we are being positive and loving when we are not being truthful and loving people, as Jesus calls and commands us to love. The inconvenient truth is called hell.

We just described the wonderful offer that the Lord Jesus makes to every individual throughout time. However, if one rejects that offer of forgiveness for their sin, they are then required to pay the penalty for their sin for eternity in a place that Jesus describes with vivid detail—hell.

No other biblical person spends more time and detail warning all people what hell is like. Jesus, unlike any other, spends the most time— with stories and graphic detail of why and what hell is like. As a side note, the writer believes that we are doing people a grave injustice by not telling what Jesus said regarding the consequence of their choice to reject His offer of love. The Bible is very clear that it is not God's will that any should perish (in hell), but that all come to repentance.[141]

A sample picture is found in Matthew's gospel. Jesus states: "They will throw them into the blazing furnace, where there will be weeping and gnashing of teeth."[142] In another discourse by Jesus, He describes this horrific place with a long list of sinners that did not choose to receive Him and follow Him. Jesus states: "They will be consigned to the fiery lake of burning sulfur. This is the second death."[143] As one can see, this place is eternally horrific and can be avoided if we choose to receive Christ's offer of forgiveness.

Many people believe that it is wrong to speak of hell and the details given to us in the Bible. They feel that it is "inappropriate" to scare people with the prospect of hell. Obviously, Jesus did not share that opinion. The author believes that integrity demands full disclosure when communicating the gospel of grace. We have a duty to tell everyone that if they choose to reject Christ's supreme sacrifice for them, they will consign themselves to that eternal place (a very real place) that Jesus called hell.

As a young boy, the author remembers that a visiting preacher came to preach at the church he was attending, Calvary Baptist Church, in Bay Shore, NY. The preacher was very graphic in his description of hell, and it left a very powerful impression on him. The writer was only six years old, but old enough to understand that he did not have to go to that place because Jesus died on the cross for him and his sins, because He loved him. Then at home during family devotions, during prayer on our knees, he prayed to Jesus, "I don't want to go to hell; please come into my heart." Childlike faith was all it took to receive the gracious gift of Christ. It is so simple a child can receive the message and have his name written in heaven and a place reserved for him!

What about you?

ENDNOTES

1. Antioxidant Revolution by Kenneth H. Cooper, M.D. is one of many books he has written on nutrition and exercise. He is recognized as a leader in these fields.
2. Hosea 4:6
3. Luke 7:35 NLT
4. Younger, by Sara Gottfried, M.D. This is the thesis of the book. She has great credentials from MIT and Harvard Medical School.
5. The Blue Zones by Dan Buettner. Please see page 68 for complete quote.
6. Ibid, p. xx
7. Ibid., p. 142
8. Ibid p. 145
9. Ibid. p. 147
10. Ibid p.228
11. Younger by Sara Gottfried, M.D. p. 14
12. 1 Corinthians 3:16
13. 1 Corinthians 6:19-20
14. The Healthier Temple Series by Ben Waller, presented to RAMBF.
15. LifeExtension page 8 October 2017

16. Ibid
17. Ibid. page 9
18. Fast Food Genocide p. 277 by Joel Fuhrman, M.D. Accidents are the leading cause of death with children under 15.
19. Life Extension October 2017 p.10
20. David Perlmuttter, M.D., FACN, is a board-certified neurologist and a leader in the field of complementary medicine. As cited from an interview on CBN with Dr. Pat Robertson, 3/31/2017.
21. Fast Food Genocide p. 93-94
22. Genesis 1:29 (NET)
23. The Antioxidant Revolution, by Dr. Kenneth Cooper, Introduction of book jacket.
24. Ibid. page 35
25. The Perricone Promise, p. 46
26. Fast Food Genocide by Joel Fuhrman, MD. p. 44
27. Healing Children Naturally, by Michael Savage, Ph.D. Dr. Savage cites many health and lifestyle issues that can be changed remarkably by food selection.
28. Fast Food Genocide by Joel Fuhrman, M.D. p. 83
29. Fast Food Genocide by Joel Fuhrman, M.D. p.84
30. CBN 700 Club TV interview November 2017
31. Fast Food Genocide by Joel Fuhrman, M.D. p. 84
32. Ephesians 5:18
33. Younger by Sara Gottfried, M.D. p. 86
34. 1 Timothy 6:17d
35. Younger by Dr. Sara Gottfried, M.D. p. 86. Gottfried lists many additives that are added to conventional wines that are not beneficial to our health. Frankly, the types of additives that she cites are quite

alarming!

36. The Better Brain Book by David Perlmutter, M.D. Dr. Perlmutter is a nationally recognized neurologist who recommends no more than two 3-ounce glasses daily. p.84

37. Interview, CBN 700 Club 3/2020

38. Ibid., 4/2020

39. Ibid., 4/2020

40. Interview, CBN 700 Club 6/2020

41. Younger by Dr. Sara Gottfried, M.D. p.88.

42. Ibid., p.88

43. Archives of Internal Medicine 160, no. 18 (2000) 2749-55. Ibid. p.88

44. We will discuss this further later in the Soul section of the book!

45. Olson RL, Brush CJ, Ehmann PJ, et al. A randomized trial of aerobic exercise on cognitive control in major depression, Clin. Neuro-physiol. 2017; 128(6):903-13.

46. Liu PZ, Nusslock R. Exercise Mediated Neurogenesis in the Hippocampus via BDNF Front Neurosci. 2918; 12:52.

47. LifeExtension July 2018. P. 81

48. Journal of Clinical Lipidol, 2018 Feb24.

49. LifeExtension Disease Prevention and Treatment Fifth Edition 130 Evidence-Based Protocols to Combat the Diseases of Aging Based on Thousands of Scientific Articles and the Clinical Experience of Physicians from Around the World

50. Life Extension Magazine, Omega-3 Fatty Acids Increase Brain Volume. August 2010. By Julius Goepp,

M.D.

51. Ibid, Julius Goepp, M.D.

52. 700 Club medical news report, by Lorie Johnson 10 April 2019

53. Hibbeln JR, Davis JM, Steer C, et al. Maternal seafood consumption in pregnancy and neurodevelopmental outcomes in childhood (ALSPAC study): an observational cohort study. Lancet. 2007 Feb 17; 369(9561):578-85.

54. O'Brien JS, Sampson EL. Lipid composition of the normal human brain: gray matter, white matter, and myelin. J Lipid Res. 1965 Oct;6(4):537-44. As cited by Julius Goepp, MD in LifeExtension August 2010

55. Julius Goepp, M.D. Life Extension Omega-3 Fatty Acids Increase Brain Volume August 2010.

56. Life Extension "How Much Fish Oil is in Your Blood?" by William Faloon March 2007

57. The two IFOS brands that are recommended are: LifeExtension Highly Purified Fish Oil 800 544 4440 or www.LifeExtension.com And Carlson Norwegian The Very Finest Fish Oil 888 234 5656 www.carlson-labs.com

58. LifeExtensions has drawing stations locally throughout the US through their membership program, which is very convenient and many times much cheaper than going through your provider. Additionally, many times they (L.E.) use the same lab company that your doctor uses. LifeExtension.com/HealthyU. 1 888 672 4352

59. www.smartypantsvitamins.com/ and www.olly.com/contact/

60. Matthew 16:26
61. The author highly recommends "Mere Christianity" and "Screwtape Letters," both by C.S. Lewis.
62. 1 Peter 2:11
63. The 5 R's were originally developed by Jon Eargle and taken from the book Healing on the Inside by him. They have been modified for use for by Constance R. Borden, Psy.D., L.C.P. of Borden Psychological Services, P.A.
64. John 10:10
65. John 10:10
66. 2 Corinthians 10:5
67. 1 Corinthians 10:13
68. Ephesians 6:10
69. Luke 10:19-20
70. 2 Corinthians 10:3-4
71. Matthew 4:4
72. Romans 12:
73. James 4:7
74. 1 Thessalians 5:16-18
75. Psalm 8:2
76. Psalm 22:3
77. Philippians 4:9
78. Hebrews 13:15
79. Hebrews 13:8
80. 2 Timothy 2:15
81. Matthew 4:4 It is written is in the perfect tense in Greek, meaning that it is a past action or statement with enduring and continuous results. The Greek work panti can also be translated "each or all word that comes."

82. Mark 11:23
83. Hebrews 4:12a
84. Hebrews 6:18b
85. Jeremiah 23:29
86. Proverbs 18:21
87. Luke 21:11
88. The Blue Zones by Dan Buettner page 149
89. John 14:27
90. Acts 13:22
91. 1 Corinthians 10:31
92. John 13:17
93. Mark 1:35
94. Psalm 5:3
95. Psalm 16:11 NET
96. Psalm 34:8
97. Medical report on CBN December 2018
98. Ibid
99. Ibid
100. Ibid
101. Mark 11:25 and Matthew 18:34-35
102. Ephesians 4:30-32
103. 1 Thessalonians 5:19 NIV and NET, respectively
104. 1 Thessalonians 5:20-21a
105. Acts 1:8
106. Hebrews 13:8
107. Hebrews 11:6
108. John 14:3
109. Ephesians 2:8-10
110. Mark 3:21 and James 4:14
111. Philippians 2:12-13
112. 2 Corinthians 5:10

113. 1 Corinthians 3:12-15
114. The 700 Club, April 2018
115. Revelation 22:12
116. 1 Corinthians 9:24-25
117. Theological Dictionary of the New Testament
Volume VII pages 631-632
118. James 1:12
119. 1 Peter 5:4
120. 1 Thessalonians 2:19-20
121. 1 Corinthians 9:24
122. 1 Corinthians 9:24, NLT
123. 2 Timothy 4:7
124. 2 Timothy 4:8
125. 1 Corinthians 3:13-15
126. Robert Jeffress, Perfect Ending (Worthy Publishing2014) p.195. Dr. Jeffress also cites Joe L. Wall, Going for the Gold (Chicago: Moody Press, 1991), p.9-10.
127. Matthew 3:17
128. Ibid 25:21
129. Robert Jeffress, Perfect Ending (Worthy Publishing 2014) p. 195
130. Matthew 25:21
131. Robert Jeffress, Perfect Ending (Worthy Publishing 2014) p.196
132. The Hebrew English Lexicon Brown, Driver, Briggs pp.524-25.
133. Psalm 119:89
134. Ecclesiastes 3:11b
135. Psalm 139: 13-14
136. John 6:35

137. Revelation 3:20
138. Revelation 21:1-5
139. John 14:2
140. The Problem of Pain by C.S. Lewis, Touchstone Edition 1996
141. 2 Peter 3:9
142. Matthew 13:42
143. Revelation 21:8